What the Church Never Told Me about Dating

What the CHURCH Never Told ME about DATING

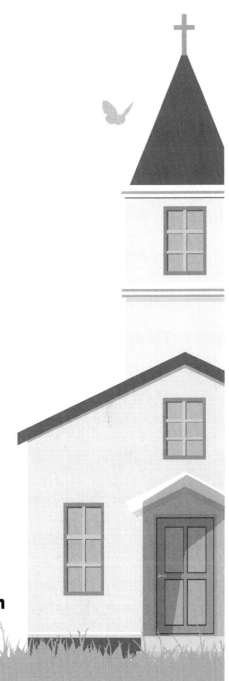

Adam Folsom
Atlanta, GA

Adam Folsom Publishing

Copyright © 2017

ISBN-13: 978-0692833148
ISBN-10: 0692833145

To Mom and Dad

You are the best parents on the planet.
I'm sorry it was "awkward" when we
edited the sex chapter together.

Contents

Section 4 - The New Game Plan for Dating

Introduction

Heartbreak

It's 3:21 a.m., I just woke up panicked! All that was rolling around in my head was painful. I liked her so much. I loved her. My heart was in pain and racing at the same time. I realized this was going to be another night of waking up every few hours, seemingly unable to control my emotions. I liked sleeping in, but now just getting a few hours of rest would be a miracle. I thought, "What has led me to this point?"

I had found a girl that I thought was "the one." On one of our early dates I took her to a Christian concert. During the intermission we were wading through the crowd and I grabbed her hand. For most of the rest of that night I didn't let go. Natalie seemed to be everything I needed. We fit so well together. If I was weak in an area she was often very strong, and vice versa. I even joked with friends that when we hugged, her head fit perfectly under my chin.

One Saturday we met friends at an Atlanta Braves baseball game. When we were walking back to the car I opened her door for her, which prompted the SUV full of girls near us to yell out, "Precious!"

We both laughed.   Earlier in the day we had talked about it.   We both wanted to have Christ involved in our relationship, so we were going to pray out loud together that day.   Sitting in the driver's seat seemed as good a time as any, so I said, "Let's pray." We both then prayed out loud. The prayers were awkward and were not anything grand, but what it did was invite the Lord of all into our relationship. That was the first time I had ever made it a priority in a relationship to pray together on a regular basis out loud.

When I brought Natalie home to meet my parents, we ate dinner and played a game of Uno (later that night she started the phone conversation with her mom, "I played the most intense game of Uno ever!"). Natalie brought flowers for my Mom, and an apple pie for dessert. Dad was stuffing his face with his piece and saying, "This is the best apple pie I have ever tasted!" He really did mean it.

At that moment I had thought, "This might be it. I might never date another person again." That was a big moment for me: understanding that this could very well be the woman I would spend the rest of my life with. And I was content with my decision. Obviously, we had more in common than great apple pie. We had good conversations, shared values, and a look in her eyes that I clearly had her heart. (Dad ate the rest of the pie that night while I was taking her home.)

But soon the problems started. Not enough time for each other, issues from our pasts, and, as is often the case, other guys tried to crowd into the picture. It felt like I was going through a car crash that I didn't know how to stop. Finally, after a couple of weeks of bad communication and frustration, it ended. I swung by her house and we both knew what was about to happen. There were no accusations, no tears, and no yelling. We had both loved each other and neither of us knew why we couldn't make it work. I didn't know how to fix our problems, or that some of them even existed.

In the restless nights that followed I wondered, "Why were two people who loved God and who loved each other not able to make it?"

Stats

Most of us dating today are living in a world totally different from that of our parents. Many of our parents married young, in their early 20s. Today, the average age of a first marriage is 28.[1] In the new normal of getting married later, people become friends and have pseudo families. This is reflected in many modern tv shows. *Seinfeld*, *New Girl*, and *The Big Bang Theory* portray what the majority of young adults are experiencing. Friends are taking the place of a

---

1   https://www.census.gov/hhes/families/files/graphics/MS-2.pdf

spouse, serving as the social and emotional support for the 8-10 year gap between when our parents got married and when we get married.

This time gap often means that people have a wider social circle, and often don't know the history, traits, and character of the people they may date. When people in previous generations married someone from their home town, they knew their future spouse's family and any positives or possible pitfalls. Today, people have to navigate a dating world of not knowing much history about your possible future spouse. What kind of baggage from past relationships and family issues are they bringing into their new relationship with you? Are there wounds that need to be healed?

In today's American population, about half the people dating have divorced parents. Many have dads who were not in the picture as often as they should have been, or not at all. This leads to people not having healthy relationships. Emotionally, people have often fallen in and out of love many times. How do people move past this baggage and not let it poison their future relationships? Since Christ-centered marriages are not often being modeled, how are couples supposed to know how to pray, serve, and worship God together?

What does the Bible say? The New Testament says nothing about dating. Why? Because dating is a relatively new concept. For much of history, marriages were arranged by the family. The parents were not as interested in finding love for their child as in keeping economic and political stability. This can be seen today in the book and movie *Pride and Prejudice*.

In *Pride and Prejudice*, when two people from the same background get married, the people in the community call it a "smart match." On the other hand, if they don't believe the couple to be good for each other it is because one is not in the same "station" as the other one. That may seem strange to you, but in an older world, where money didn't come and go from families as quickly, maybe it made sense. Today it would be foolish to think that money stays with families, because now people become successful based on work ethic, merit, good ideas, ambition, and often blessings from God, too.

Finally, the church's main message about today's dating world is "Don't have sex." The church rarely says what to do, just what not to do: "Don't have sex." Actually, that isn't bad advice. I agree with it. But it doesn't answer my questions: "Who should I marry? How do I find her? Other than 'Don't have sex' does God care about what I do physically?" It turns out "Don't have sex!" has been an ineffective message. A study done in 2010 showed 80% of evangelical Christian singles 18-30 had already had sex.[2] A new game plan is needed for the growing single population

2   http://religion.blogs.cnn.com/2011/09/27/why-young-christians-arent-waiting-anymore/

in the church. (Even if you are not a Jesus follower, please read on. A little help in the dating area is always useful.)

After about ten years of triumphs, heartbreaks, and lessons learned I have discovered a new game plan to help with the second most important question any Christian will ever answer: "Who should I marry?"

My Introduction

My name is Adam Folsom. I grew up in a very positive environment. My parents are still married. They never let on to me about any problems that were big. They argued, of course, about typical relationship problems, but there were never any big arguments with slamming doors and storming out. They took me to church almost every time the doors were open (yes, I was a Sunday morning, Sunday night, and Wednesday night churchgoer for years). Whenever I go back to my hometown, I sometimes hear people joke that they remember when I was a kid disrupting church in some way. When I was seven years old, I remember standing up in front of the congregation of our little country church to be baptized. I told my story about how I put my trust in Jesus. One of the pastors, who was a close family friend, shouted out, "Sounds like a preacher to me!" And everyone laughed.

There is another side of me that the people on Sunday morning often don't see. One day when I was about three I was walking with my Dad, and I threw a rock at a big garage door. He told me, "Don't throw any more rocks at the garage door," as any good parent would do. I took another rock in my hand, ran up to the door and started tapping on it. I knew where the line was, and I was pushing it. That is how I have lived my life. I know where the line is and push it absolutely as much as I can. There is something in me that gets a rush when staying slightly within the lines, but breaking the spirit of the rules. I think there is a bit of that in all of us. I don't like following rules just because that is what someone in a church thinks. I want to follow a rule because it was given to us by God to follow. I don't want to go through life doing this or that because that is what I "ought" to do. I want to go through life living freely and doing what God has called me to do.

Looking back now I realize I was fortunate. Somehow I grew up slow. In high school I was more concerned with sports than chasing girls. I liked them, but they seemed to be more trouble than they were worth. Getting all dressed up and spending a lot of money to go to a dance wasn't my idea of a good time at age 16. I did go to several of the dances though, and the pictures show me as nervous as can be. My first homecoming dance I have a picture of me wearing a coca-cola tie, standing awkwardly with a one-foot gap between my date and me.

On top of that, the parents of the girl who I often wanted to date were incredibly strict and scary. I had to have her home way earlier than everyone else. There were never any deep feelings there, so other than a very occasional date, I stayed single.

Then I went off to college. I had played ice hockey ever since we moved to Michigan when I was 10, and, after a tryout I was offered a place on the Hope College hockey team. Little did I know this would open up more doors with girls in the next four years than I could imagine. Hockey is a big deal in Michigan. Each person on my team got a hooded sweatshirt with his number on the sleeve, and by wearing it everyone knew this person played on the team. Once I got mine, I realized that most girls on campus wanted to wear one. It showed status and popularity. It didn't matter that I didn't play much. I was on the team. I had status. Freshman year I had a big time. If it wasn't for Dad really pushing me to stay away from alcohol it would have been too big a time.

I took a religion class that required us to attend a Catholic Mass. I walked in the church door and saw Abby O'Brien, standing by the door about to go into the service. She was in my mind and my friends' minds one of the hottest (Christian circles would say "prettiest") girls in our freshman class. I walked up to her and said, "I'm Adam. I don't have much of a Catholic background. Do you know what you are doing here?" She knew who I was and we sat through the service together. At one point I was feeling good about doing the sign of the cross and I could see it was about to be done. So I tried to follow everyone else and apparently did something wrong because I quickly ended up with her elbow in my side. Then after some laughing and coaching by her I was able to get it the next time. We walked back to campus together and had a good time.

A couple of days later (I'm about to date myself) I picked up a phone with a cord attached to the wall, looked through a paper directory, and called Abby for a dinner date on Friday. We went to dinner, then had coffee, and then caught a movie. (This stacking events one after the other has become a trademark of mine. I call it the marathon date. I ask a girl to do one thing earlier in the day. Then if it goes well I ask her to do something else. And keep the events stacking one on top of the other. That way if it goes poorly you just end the date early, no problem, but if it goes well a marathon date gets past the small talk and accelerates the relationship.) We had a great time. She sent me an email right afterward saying she did. I talked to her a couple of times during exam week, and then we left for different towns for the summer. By the time she returned, she was dating someone else and that was that.

And that is pretty much how most of us date today. You date someone and get off to a promising start, but it doesn't work out. We don't have easy clear-cut partners we know God meant for us to be with. When we hear our friends talking about their "soul mate" we really wonder if there is someone like that for everyone, because there certainly hasn't been anyone like that for us. A lot of our dating stories end up like Abby O'Brien. There is potential, but then life happens. Work gets in the way. Distance gets in the way. Busyness gets in the way.

I'm glad I met these girls in high school and early college, but I didn't cry when I lost them. I certainly wish them the best. Last time I saw them, one was an Indianapolis Colts cheerleader and another was on the cover of a Colorado magazine. They were fun memories, which in the tougher times of life are always good to remember.

This book is written for the rest of us. How can we find a great partner and do what we all dream of…live happily ever after?

The Old Christian Game Plan For Dating

In the conservative Christian world I grew up in, this is how I was told to find a wife:

Cue the sappy romantic music.

My sophomore year of college, Dan lived down the hall. He had gone to high school with one of my roommates from the previous year and we quickly became best friends. He is one of the brightest guys I've ever met. A chemistry major in college, he completed med school and is now an ophthalmologist. He grew up in a church culture where scripture by memory was extremely important. In fact, he memorized almost all of the New Testament. If we were in theological debates I would often try to make a point and he would know the verse and reference I was talking about. We also watched a lot of football together. My senior year my team only won three games, so it was a grim football season.

Dan's hometown was two hours from school, so one weekend, when there was an event at his home church, we went for a visit. There was clearly a strong feeling of community at this church. I was meeting everybody. Then Dan introduced me to a girl named Sarah. She was very happy to see him, and gave him a lot of attention. I could tell there was quite a bit of attraction. On our way home, and again later that day, I brought this to his attention. He prayed about it.

Not long after the semester was over, Dan talked to his Dad about possibly dating Sarah. Then, because there was so much good community in that church, he discussed it with Sarah's dad. I remember his phone call, "I'm going on a date with Sarah this weekend!" Which was followed at the end of the weekend with, "I went on a date with Sarah! Other than a very embarrassing spaghetti spill, and a trip to Meijer for stain remover, it went really well." I laughed hard. Knowing Dan, I knew this was probably going to end in marriage. Neither he nor Sarah had really dated anyone before this, the community support was incredible, and they cared for each other.

Sure enough, two years later I had moved to Atlanta and was flying into Dan's home town for his church wedding in Michigan. Everyone's family was there. They all got along. There was no yelling. No bridezilla. There was a period where the families who had known each other for decades were praying for the couple. I thought, while standing as a groomsman, "This is ideal. Dan is getting a fantastic girl. They have similar beliefs and their relationship is Christ-centered. They both have very little bad baggage they are bringing into the relationship. Both families are getting along and care for each other."

I still visit Dan once or twice a year, and whenever I see him I often ask, "Marriage looks easy for you?" He usually responds, "It is!" Of all my friends, Dan and Sarah have by far the strongest marriage. They get along well. They support each other. Yes, they do have issues to work through, but they have a positive relationship. It truly is ideal.

I can just see the Youth Pastors of America and the world eating up this story. I was taught growing up that Dan's experience was what you should shoot for. Marrying a girl from the church...just sitting together on the front porch and living happily ever after. The only big decision would be, "Should we have the reception in the Church's Fellowship Hall without dancing, or at the school gym and get a DJ?"

Don't get me wrong, I would sign up for this situation. I think most of us would. But guess what? I was in high school and it didn't happen. I was in college and it didn't happen. I was out of college and it didn't happen. I was 25 and it didn't happen. I was 30 and still single. What about the rest of us? What about those of us who don't easily find Mr. or Miss. Right? How do we date? How do we find people to be in relationships with? No one ever gave us a manual.

Section One

Red Flag Warnings

"From the errors of others,

a wise man corrects his own."

Publilius Syrus

Chapter 1

Dad Issues

After my first year of college, I was working during the summer at a water park in Kentucky. (I have family in the area and my parents owned a small condo on the lake.) I figured if I was going to have to make some money I might as well sit in the sun and hang out with lots of young people. My very first day that summer I was waiting for the park to open when a girl was strolling toward me over a small walking bridge. I remember it vividly like it was in slow motion. We struck up a conversation about where we were from and what kind of cars we drove. She said her name was Kelly. Then the park opened, the crowds came in, and we went our separate ways.

I wouldn't say I knew right away that Kelly was going to be someone special. She was dating someone else at the time. But about midway through that summer she became available, and I asked her if she wanted to grab dinner after work. She immediately said, "Of course!" I had intended for the two of us, sweaty from a day in the sun, to go straight from work to somewhere casual and eat. I quickly realized that she intended to go home and freshen up. It was becoming a bigger deal than I was expecting.

We were sitting at The Oasis restaurant having a good conversation when Kelly said, "My mom doesn't usually let me stay out this late on a weekday, but she made an exception!" My next question was, "What about your dad?" She said, "My dad is in jail." She made that statement matter-of-factly and we just moved on. Later that evening we sat by the lake and had a fun first date. (The first song I ever recorded, *By the Lakeside*, was about this experience.)

Kelly and I began dating after that; we had a great end of the summer together. I later found out that her dad was in prison for drugs. She didn't have a relationship with him at all. And he wasn't just busted for smoking pot; he was into meth and other hard drugs. Despite this, and most of her family avoiding church, Kelly woke up on Sundays and went to church on her own. She might not have been a super regular attender, but for a 17-year-old to make that step on her own impressed me very much, then and now.

Less than a month later I headed back to Michigan to begin my sophomore year at Hope College. Before I left, Kelly gave me a present. It was an old stuffed-animal chicken. I looked at it somewhat unimpressed, but then she said, "This is the only thing I have that my father ever gave me. I just know you are going to go off and do something great someday. I want you to someday look at that chicken and think of me." What a statement! She gave me her most prized possession. I was blown away then, and frankly the older I get, I'm even more blown away. Outside of my parents I don't believe anyone has ever given me a gift where they gave so much. Also, in her statement to me, she became the first girl to really believe in me, and what I could accomplish. When I am dating someone who believes in me, I feel I can accomplish anything.

For the next two years we were a typical young dating couple, regularly breaking up and getting back together, trying to date and live in different states most of the year.

One thing was clear: there was no dad in the picture. There was no dad to send her back upstairs to change when she was wearing something way too revealing for a teenager. So the guys she attracted often were not well intentioned. There was no dad to tell her how valuable she was and not to let someone treat her poorly. There was no dad to tell her how proud he was that she was the Top All-American Cheerleader her senior year of high school. There was no father to protect her. There was no father to help her to resist peer pressure. Her dad wasn't there to yell at me when I wasn't treating her as well as she should have been treated. Her dad was never there to say, "I love you."

Eventually, because of the distance and fighting, we broke up and she moved on. It was not long after that she was married and having a kid. I was shocked. I was only 20 at the time and knew I wasn't mature enough to be married...and certainly not mature enough to be a dad. I still felt like a kid myself. I couldn't imagine going to school and raising one.

I'm not trying to make anyone feel bad who was (or is) a parent in a marriage they may have jumped into too soon. I certainly don't want to put anyone down for events that have happened in the past. I have seen so many girls similar to Kelly and I think they are doing a better job of being a parent at a young age than I could. I have watched from a distance as Kelly has raised her kids, and am very proud of the job she has done. She made her road very tough by her actions, but she has made it through college, a masters program, and is now a kindergarten teacher. All while having to manage a household and two kids. She has really turned her family situation around. I believe with God that any of us can turn our situations around as well.

But the fact remains that the "Dad Problem" is a big one. Inevitably, other girls I have dated, and guy friends I have known since then, have had some kind of dad situation to overcome. It usually comes out quickly in conversation. A couple of years ago, I was driving a new friend to a singles event at church. I was asking him general questions, and he told me his dad had just taken his life a few weeks prior. Needless to say he was still trying to put the pieces together.

I was driving a girl home from the airport (why do I seem to have these conversations in my car while driving someone somewhere?!?!). She was telling me about her family and how her dad had just really "gone off the deep end." He came to visit her and was hitting on her friends, and trying to one up the guys who were around as well. It was a disaster of a situation and she was trying to make sense of everything.

Important fact: When the father is causing problems, it creates a fog for everyone in the family. It's tough for the family to know what to do next.

I've learned that if a girl has a "Dad Problem" it comes up quickly in conversation. Whenever I have tried to date girls who are broken inside because of their father, I have never had a successful healthy relationship. It is always stressful with lots of fighting. I really believe they are giving me everything they can, but at that moment—while they are trying to put the pieces back together—they don't have enough to give themselves, much less to someone they are dating.

My nature is to avoid obstacles and just plow through, but after being hurt a couple of times, I am much more cautious when I hear a girl talking about her dad not being there. That is a red flag warning for me. I was recently at a luncheon when I was talking to a pretty girl about where she grew up. "Why did you move so much?" I asked. "Well, my dad wanted to go to seminary," she said, "but it turned out he was a highly functioning alcoholic, so we had to move a few times." I was very sympathetic with her, but it made me think. "I wonder if she is still broken, or if the pieces have been put back together?" So instead of asking her for a date, I sat back and watched. (After watching her in our group for a few months, I saw that she was a fantastic girl with Christ as her anchor. She was indeed very dateable.)

The "Dad Problem" is one area where, admittedly, I have had it easy. My dad was and is regularly telling me he loves me and is proud of me. He was usually at my games growing up. He always provided. He was always at church. He has prayed for the sick and they have recovered. He lives his life at home the same way he portrays himself to other people. He's not a hypocrite. I watched him tithe when we had very little, and now he has a lot (and still tithes). I watched him and mom go up for prayer when they had a tough stretch in their marriage, and they are still married 30+ years. I watched him leave a tenured job as a professor at Murray State University to pursue other dreams; today he is a best selling author and speaker (and once again a tenured professor). It's easier for me to go through life pursuing my dreams because I have a stable, supportive father.

The type of relationship God wants to have with us is similar to that of an earthly father. Repeatedly throughout scripture, God is referred to as a Father. Even people who aren't Christians probably know the prayer that Christ taught us to pray, "Our FATHER in heaven...."

For some of you, that thought scares you away from God. You might say, "My father was terrible! He certainly isn't someone I want to follow and grow closer to." I think I understand where you are coming from. Much of what we think about God comes from what we think about our dads. If you grew up with a dad who was loving and generous, that is probably what you think about God. If you grew up with a dad who was a scorekeeper, always telling you how wrong you were, you probably think God is out to get you as well. If you had a dad who wasn't there, you probably have a harder time believing that God is always there for you. I'll say it again, much of what you think about God comes from what you think about your dad.

Some of you may be thinking, "That's true Adam, I've had a tough situation, but what can I do about it now?"

First, I think you just need to realize there is a gap between what your father should have been, and what he was. God didn't intend for your dad to be a problem. God wanted the best for you. Even if your earthly father was a problem, it isn't God's fault.

There still might be a gap with you and your dad's relationship, and it will affect you negatively. It is a big deal!

Often when guys and girls have father issues, they date continually, having the same problems over and over. They will say things like, "All the guys I date are idiots." Or "All the girls I date are crazy." Guess what? You're attracting them and picking them. Stop it! Understand you probably have some "Daddy baggage," and it is affecting how you dress, how you act, who you choose to date, and how you live. Start picking people who value God, themselves, and you. Start hanging around people who can help you put the pieces back together. Go to a small group, a counselor, a pastor, or find a mentor who can help you work through these issues.

Second, the good news is you have another father. A Perfect Father. "Your heavenly Father is perfect" (Matthew 5:48). I would recommend picking up a Bible and learning about Him. Your life isn't perfect, but there is a perfect Father, with no faults, who is loving you unconditionally. I'm not saying that you have to believe everything right away, or that it will be an easy road. But I strongly believe, and I'm sure if you were honest with yourself that you would agree: Your life will improve the more you plug into, listen to, cast your cares on, receive unconditional love from, and pray with a perfect loving heavenly Father.

I did a little digging and this is what your perfect heavenly Father has to say about you:

• "Your eyes saw my unformed body; all the days ordained for me were written in your book before one of them came to be" (Psalm 139:16). You are not an accident. God saw your first heartbeat. Can you imagine that? He was waiting and saw you before you were born, and saw that moment when your tiny heart first began to beat. And He loved you.

• "See how very much our Father loves us, for he calls us his children, and that is what we are! But the people who belong to this world don't recognize that we are God's children because they don't know him" (1 John 3:1 NLT).

• "'For I know the plans I have for you,' declares the Lord, 'plans to prosper you and not to harm you, plans to give you hope and a future'" (Jeremiah 19:11 NIV). That's what a good Father does; he sets you up to succeed.

• "This is love: not that we loved God, but that He loved us and sent his Son as an atoning sacrifice for our sins" (1 John 4:10). God loved you so much, yes YOU, that he sent Jesus to die on the cross so that he can be in a Father/child relationship with you.

• "The Lord himself goes before you and will be with you; he will never leave you nor forsake you. Do not be afraid; do not be discouraged" (Deuteronomy 31:8 and Hebrews 13:5 NIV). A more literal translation from the original Greek would be, "I will not, I will not, I will not let you down, leave you in the lurch, leave you destitute, leave you in straits and helpless, abandon you."[1] Let that soak in. Your Heavenly Father will never, never, never leave you. Never.

• "Even if my father and mother abandon me, the Lord will hold me close" (Psalm 27:10 NLT). No matter what has happened with your family in the past, God the FATHER is holding you close.

• "For God so loved the world that he gave his one and only Son, that whoever believes in him shall not perish but have eternal life" (John 3:16 NIV). Even one of the most popular verses in the Bible says it. He loves you![2]

The good news is that I have seen many people from rough family environments plug into their Perfect Heavenly Father and turn their situations around.

Lord, I pray that all the people reading this would understand the love their Heavenly Father has for them. That they would believe the truth of His love and dismiss the lies from the enemy that they are not

---

1   Kenneth S. Wuest, *Hebrews in the Greek New Testament* (Grand Rapids: Erdmanns, 1947), 234.
2   Read more verses about God being our Perfect Father:
1 John 4:16, Matthew 7:11, Romans 8:39, Luke 12:24.

enough, not loved, or not deeply cared for. I pray that they would fully understand their value and why God paid the enormous price of sending his Son to die on the cross for our sins. I know and pray God is putting all the pieces in your life together and His plans are for your good. Even if it is sometimes hard for you to believe this, please Lord, be real to them and let them know your love for them.

Red Flag Warning #1:

1. If you grew up with a father who was absent, or who wasn't loving and protective, it does affect your actions and how you live your life. For help, find a mentor who has gone before you on this road, or look for a faith-based counselor.

2. You may need to take a break from dating while you are putting these pieces back together. You might not have enough love and peace to give to yourself, much less to someone else.

3. If you are interested in dating someone, and if he or she has unresolved Dad Problems, make sure these problems are being taken care of, and possibly take a break from dating if needed.

4. Understand that God is a Perfect Father. When you plug into God the Father, what He says about you and how He loves you, then you will begin to heal.

Chapter 2

Put a Period on Previous Relationships

In previous relationships, even after they were clearly over, I always thought they still had a chance. I am naturally optimistic, even if the odds are against me. If I want something, I believe with God and hard work I can achieve it. So when a relationship is over, in my head I think that with enough prayer, or if I just show her some other aspect of my life, this could still work out. Most of us have done it. We hold on to something that isn't there.

The ending of my relationship with Natalie is an example of this. (Yes, the same bad breakup I described in the first pages of this book.) We dated for months. In fact, we sent each other 4065 text messages (that was the actual total from my phone's counter!). We sat up talking on the dock until 2 a.m. My picture was on her dresser, and her mom downloaded my music and thought I was a really good singer. Natalie got a good look. It didn't work. At night I could either lie in bed and stare at the ceiling fan feeling sorry for myself, and be angry at Natalie, or I could put a period on it and move on.

I finally decided I was not wasting any more time. Holding on to something that isn't working is stressful. I am a stress non-eater. In the last three weeks I had lost 10 pounds, and I wasn't overweight to begin with. I had to force myself to eat. It wasn't healthy for me.

So when I woke up every few hours in a panic, dwelling on the failed relationship, I told myself, "I put a period." And I started to think about other things. Colossians 3:2 says, "Set your minds and keep them set on what is above (the higher things), not on the things that are on the earth." That is often easier said than done. In order to "keep my mind set" on something other than the relationship falling apart I had to actively think about what I was thinking about. When my thoughts would wander I would have to force them back to sports, a tv series on Netflix, or, if I was feeling ultra-holy that day, a Bible verse.

The first couple of days and nights not a lot else happened other than I had to reset my mind about every five minutes. I would be sitting at a restaurant and looking at the empty chair next to me. This would remind me of how when she got excited she would do a little dance in her seat. Then I would have to kick myself and think about positive things again. In the mornings I used to receive a "Have a great day babe!"

text message, and now, when I looked at my phone I had to once again force my thoughts in a positive direction. It was a slow process, but as the days passed I noticed I was not dwelling on the relationship as often. I didn't have to constantly think about something to keep my mind from wandering in a bad direction. After about two weeks, I finally started to sleep better and become my old self again.

Then I pulled up Facebook. There she was right on my newsfeed, looking as wonderful as ever. The old feelings and the pain all came rushing back again. I quickly realized that was a bad choice. I once again had to go back and direct my thoughts to positive things. I stayed off social media completely. Then a friend recommended that I unfollow her from all my accounts. I did that, and now none of her life is influencing mine. If something is important I will hear about it through the grapevine, but I don't have to hear about her daily pumpkin spice latte at Starbucks on Twitter.

Some of you may be saying, "Yes, Adam, that makes sense, but what about the couples that do get back together?" To that I say, "You have watched *The Notebook* or *The Vow* too many times!" These types of movies always show the couple overcoming huge odds. If I bump into Natalie at a party in the future, and somehow we have worked through our issues, I would certainly be up for starting over again. But I'm not sitting around feeling sorry for myself waiting for that to happen. And neither should you if you are getting past somebody. Putting a period at the end of that relationship was for me—my well-being, my health, and my peace of mind. I will be in the best shape possible for my future wife if I put a period on Natalie, get myself together emotionally, and move on.

As this process was going on, I was undateable. I'm sure the girls I was talking with at the time saw it, too, and it was a red flag warning. I was broken and could barely keep myself together, much less care about someone else.

Natalie and I had a mutual friend, Jenelle, who broke up with a guy about a month before we did. She was very pretty and appealed to lots of quality guys. The guy she had been dating treated her horribly. I understood the first time or two after the breakup when I saw her that she was still a little hung up on the guy. They had dated for more than a year. Then, after I had gotten over Natalie, I was at an event with Jenelle and several other friends. I can still remember one of the guys saying, "All Jenelle talks about is her old boyfriend. I hope I don't have to talk to her." She was probably the hottest girl at the event, but she hadn't put a period on her old relationship, and the guys in the room were running in the other direction.

Sometimes feelings never quite go away. I'll occasionally hear an old song, or see an old picture, and feelings will come flooding back. That is okay. It's a natural reaction. When dating, I sometimes run into situations where I see a girl having one of these moments too. It isn't something to beat up yourself or your special someone about though. The key is not to linger.

Red Flag Warning #2:

When dealing with a failed relationship, put a period on it and move forward.

Chapter 3

Finances

Often people come up to me to talk about finances. Money is important and managing money is one of my strengths. I have worked in a corporate finance environment for nine years, and I have an embarrassing confession: Occasionally I dream about numbers and spreadsheets in Microsoft Excel. Yes, that is super lame. But money management has always come naturally to me. I know exactly how much money is in my accounts and can tell if one purchase is going to stretch me too thin.

When I was first out of college in 2007-2008, the financial collapse happened and everyone was talking about money (usually how little they had). I often heard about people losing their homes or investments. Very wisely, my church had a series on personal finances, and all of our small groups were following along with the curriculum.

One of the lessons was on debt and everyone in my small group was supposed to figure out what and how much they owed: house, car, student loans, credit cards, personal loans, everything. At the time I was just renting and the only debt I had was a small car payment—to match my small income. Most of the guys in the group were only in their late 20s or early 30s, but I was absolutely floored by the amount of debt most of them had. After undergrad, graduate school, a starter house, car, and, of course, credit cards, some owed hundreds of thousands of dollars. We were all realizing they were going to be paying large amounts on those loans for decades. I was blown away.

The guys in my small group were having to learn how to live on a budget, which wasn't always easy. We all had to cut out things we liked to do, but at the end of the series our lives were more in balance. We now had plans to control our finances, tithe, avoid debt, and save.

Soon after hearing the money series at church, I was more aware of some of my friends being derailed by debt. One of my buddies from college, for example, decided to join the Army because he had six figure student loans. He found a program that would help pay them off if he enlisted and served. I believe the life of a soldier is a noble profession, and admire those who serve our country, but I don't believe that is what my friend was called to do. He had a business degree. I remember being in classes with him, occasionally talking about his business future. He may be a great soldier, but is he called to do that?

One day I was at work and a co-worker, Kendal, who is about my age, started talking to me about her debt and student loans. She had accumulated about $100k in loans during college. That would be fine if her income was able to pay off the loan quickly, but she was making about $35,000/year, while living in a fairly expensive city, Atlanta. She had very little spare money and would be paying on the loans for decades. Every time I talked to her I couldn't get over the fact that if we got in a relationship I would be taking on her debt.

In the future, would she continue spending more than she had? I don't want a lifetime of fighting over money when I am married.

Finances, as everyone knows, are one of the top reasons for divorce today. Yet, when I ask people who haven't been married what they think about their future spouse and finances, the response is usually, "It's no big deal" or "Adam, you should focus on finding the right person, the money will take care of itself." But when I ask married people or divorced friends the same question, their response is usually the exact opposite. One friend I talked to who was married for three years, and is now divorced, said, "How a girl handles her finances is one of the first questions I ask a girl on a date, or even before we go on a date!" I can see why both sides think the way they do. Single people often want everything to be a fairy tale, but married people know first hand that how finances are handled in marriage is very important.

I remember growing up how tight things were financially in my family until I was in high school. One of my earliest memories is when my Dad vacuumed up my Mom's lip balm. (Things were so tight that Mom only bought one lip balm at a time.) I remember looking out the window outside and Dad was looking through the dirty vacuum bag to find Mom's one lip balm. Back then, even the less-than-a-dollar lip balm needed to be saved. Life is just much tougher when you are living paycheck to paycheck, and even as a kid I could feel it. Every purchase was scrutinized. There was no breathing room in my family's life; as soon as money was made, it was spent. Now that I am older, I appreciate that my family didn't go into debt in those years. They knew that things were tight and they kept an eye on the budget all the time. This caused higher stress levels for everyone. I remember bumps would come up (car repairs, taxes, medical expenses) and life for my parents would quickly get stressful.

In the last several years (especially after the money series at church), I have seen first-hand many couples get married and have financial problems soon after. They often have two incomes and yet they still struggle to keep right side up every month. They will make close to double my income, live in the same area of town that I do, but seem to live always stressed out about bills. But other couples I have seen take their finances seriously, do very well, and their lives are much simpler and happier. The pressure of living paycheck to paycheck is gone. The stress of debt is gone. Life is more peaceful.

Back to Kendal. A couple of years later I learned that she was looking for a new place to live. Kendal was probably making more money now and many of her friends were moving into nicer apartments or condos. I soon found out she was moving into a cheap 500 square-foot efficiency apartment. When I asked her about it she said, "This is going to allow me to pay down my student loans faster." I was impressed. She saw her problem, she made a plan, and she was getting out of debt. In my mind she had become dateable again.

I don't believe anyone is past redemption in any area of life, but someone who is carrying lots of debt is carrying lots of baggage into a relationship. Just like with any baggage, it needs to be sorted out.

If I were interested in going further in a relationship with a girl, and if she had a lot of debt and was regularly living beyond her means, I would consider her undateable. Not that she would be that way forever, but until she had a plan, and was shrinking her debt, I would pass.

If you have too much debt, get a plan, get a book. There are several sermon series and books that show you exactly what you need to know. The sermon series I went through with my small group was Andy Stanley's *Balanced.* I highly recommend it. Several people I know have also benefited from Dave Ramsey's books.

Every week, I go to the ATM and pull out $100. That cash is what I have to spend on food/entertainment/clothes for the week. That is what I can afford. When the money gets low, I'm trying to eat at my parents' place for a free meal (Thanks, Mom!). When I have a big date or something going on that week, I am sure to spend less in other areas. Sometimes I miss the mark, but I have a goal to shoot for.

There are several good ways to handle your money, so find one that works for you.

Red Flag Warning #3:

1. If you have large amounts of debt and bad financial habits, you are setting yourself up for big problems in your marriage. Get a financial plan and stick with it. Then you will have a more peaceful life for yourself and your future spouse.

2. If you are attracted to someone who has financial problems, don't get too close until he or she figures out those problems. You and your future partner need to control spending. You aren't just marrying each other. You are combining both financial situations as well.

Chapter 4

Other Red Flag Warnings

It was a cool night in Atlanta when Chelsea and I went for a drive. We swung by Starbucks to have a warm beverage and were driving around different neighborhoods. We were having a fun evening, when we drove down a street and the atmosphere in the car changed. Chelsea said, "I used to nanny for a house down that street," as she pointed to a cross street we were passing. After a minute or two of silence, I awkwardly started talking about the weather and different topics. The atmosphere was still tense. I figured something happened with that nanny situation, but I didn't feel it was my place to ask about it.

Finally, about 15 minutes later we were still driving around and Chelsea said, "So back there. I was a nanny for a kid named Michael for over a year. His parents were divorced and I watched him when he was at his dad's." She went on to tell me more about the family situation and how great a kid Michael was. She continued, "Then one day I was dropping Michael off at his dad's house, and he needed to pay me for the last couple of weeks of nannying. So the Dad and I went into the house so he could write me a check. That's when he attacked me. He tried to rape me. I did eventually get away before anything too much happened, and left."

Whoa! I was not expecting that. This was big stuff. I was under control, but there was a big piece of me that just wanted to turn the car around, knock on that guy's door, and do a public service and give the guy the beating of a lifetime. Chelsea and I spent the next half hour talking about his assault and how she dealt with the trauma.

Even though this attack occurred several years ago, Chelsea was still dealing with it, and now I was too. Of course, I never thought any less of her. She had been through a traumatic experience that was not her fault. I was irate when I thought about this guy. He was a prominent leader in town. I kept thinking, "Someday I will be sitting at the same table as this monster at a charity event, and what will I say? What will I do?"

Finally, one night I realized, "I need to figure this out and get past it." I didn't want to give that monster any more of my time, thoughts, joy, peace, or future. He had already caused enough problems. I wasn't going to let him steal anymore from me. So I opened the notes app on my phone and started typing a prayer. I prayed for Chelsea to be able to forgive and move on, and I prayed the same for myself. I prayed neither of us would ever see this guy again, and that he would never hurt anyone again. A few days later I read that prayer with Chelsea, and at least for me, I was able to move on.

Everyone's closet has skeletons, old bad/tough/ messy experiences from their past. Some, the victim could not prevent, like in the story above, but some are totally self-inflicted.

After more than ten years of dating, I have seen quite a few skeletons rear their ugly heads. Some had been dealt with, and the person had moved on; in other cases, the skeletons were still causing problems.

Lust

One of the most common skeletons I have seen many guys (and girls) struggle with is pornography. It is easy to conceal and today, with the internet, is very accessible. Everyone must get lust under control or it will flare up. It might seem like a small problem now, but it has the potential to cause large problems in the future. What do you think your future wife would do if you were viewing porn regularly? She would probably feel like you betrayed her trust, and she certainly wouldn't respect you more for it. Break the habit now, before it grows and consumes more of your mind! Believe me I understand it's difficult. Everyone battles it. 2 Timothy 2:22 says, "Flee also youthful lusts." Don't accommodate them: flee from them.[1]

We have to constantly be thinking about where we are looking. I will feel like I am doing a good job and then some girl wearing a bright pink sports bra and tight yoga shorts will be running on the treadmill right in front of me. I sometimes have to get off and go to another machine. That situation might not be a problem for everyone, but for me, I need to get out of there. You have to know yourself and put yourself in positive situations. I subscribe to many of the movie channels with my cable package. Some of the content on these channels are positive entertaining shows and movies, but other shows are inappropriate. I had a good friend over and he was flipping around the channels and said, "If I had all these channels, I would be watching shows I know I shouldn't be watching." I encouraged the guy for realizing that about himself. For whatever reason, I am not usually tempted to watch inappropriate shows or movies on tv, but for my friend they are an issue. We need to know ourselves and what is going to cause us to stumble.

If I am fighting (and mostly winning) these battles now, I will be in much better shape for myself, for any girl I am dating, and for my future wife.

---

1   64% of Christian men and 15% of Christian women say they watch porn at least once a month. See Covenanteyes.com.

Body Image

One of the saddest realizations I have had in my adult life is that most people are insecure about their bodies. I might change a couple of things about myself (my ears are uneven), but overall I give God a thumbs up on how I was made. I was naive about body image until I was a sophomore in college and all the girls in my dorm had to go to a seminar on body image and eating disorders. Girls suffering from bulimia were often throwing up in the community bathroom. I was shocked. These girls had no reason to feel bad about themselves.

I have dated several girls along the way who have a negative body image as well. Even though they were very attractive, deep down they believed they were unattractive. I have also dated girls who at one time were anorexic and were putting the pieces of their lives back together. How could girls so beautiful feel so ugly?

This is what the Bible says about you: "For [God] created my inmost being; you knit me together in my mother's womb. I praise you because I am fearfully and wonderfully made; your works are wonderful, I know that full well" (Psalm 139:13-14). Stop believing the lies from the media that you need to look a certain way; most of those images are fake or photoshopped anyway.

One of the girls I knew who had anorexia was overcoming it by keeping images of photoshopped models out of her life. She rarely went on social media, she didn't have cable tv, and when I looked around her apartment I never saw a fashion magazine. She had eliminated the fake negative images and was much healthier for it.

If you are reading this and struggling, please get help! We all need a counselor at different points in our lives.

Red Flag #4:

All of us have skeletons in our closets from past problems. Besides abuse, lust, and poor body image, there are many other examples I could have used. My guess is, as you read this chapter, skeletons you need to clean out came to mind. Don't let them rattle around in your future!

Section 1
Study Questions

1. What kind of father did/do you have? Is there a gap between who your father was and who he should have been? If you need help in this area, who are you reaching out to?

2. Are there former relationships in your life that you need to put a period on to move forward? Who do you need to unfollow from your social media accounts?

3. Do you spend more money every month than you earn? How much debt do you have? Do you have a financial plan? Are you saving, investing, and tithing?

4. What are the skeletons in your closet?
   - Do you have blocks on the internet to prevent you from temptation?
   - What is the mental image you have of your body? Is it positive or negative? What does God have to say about your body and how valuable you are? (On page 43, reread Psalm 139:13-14.)
   - What area of your life do you need to turn over to God for healing?

5. Do not answer this question in a group setting: Is there someone in your life you should not date because of their Red Flag Warnings?

<u>Section Two</u>

Who Are You Listening To?

"I like to listen. I have learned a great deal from listening carefully. Most people never listen."

Ernest Hemingway

Chapter 5

Who and What Are You Listening To?

My first real job out of college in 2008 was working as a financial analyst for Popeyes Louisiana Kitchen. When I first started working for Popeyes, it had a real mom-and-pop feel. Most of the employees had worked there a long time, and people really cared about each other. It was a great place to start a career.

One thing, however, quickly became obvious: I was by far the youngest employee in the corporate office. During my second month working there, I filled out a bracket for the March Madness Basketball Tournament. Rod, the person who ran the bracket pool, would send out regular emails about who was winning and losing. Here is what he said about me in his first email:

"Adam Folsom...for those that don't know him, he's the alleged college graduate that looks more like a cast member of the Hannah Montana series. Adam spent the whole morning contacting his inner circle of fraternity brothers to conclude that Butler deserves a ticket to the elite 8. Hey rookie, thanks for the $10 and I will be leaving at 5:15 today, so be at my office to carry my bags to the car!"

Rod roasted everybody, not just me, but that gives you an idea of what it was like when I started out. Everyone treated me like I was a kid (in a lot of ways I still was).

Even the older African-American receptionist called me, in an endearing way, "Baby Adam." Until I saw the movie The Help I had no idea why she called me that (watch the movie; it's a good one).

With this mom-and-pop close-knit culture, and my youth, a lot of the older ladies in the office took it upon themselves to make sure I was taking care of myself. If I coughed, or had a headache, they would come by and make sure I was taking medicine or resting enough. Above all, they loved to ask, "Who are you dating?"

I quickly found that everyone had a different opinion about what to do or not do in dating situations. One person would say, "Call her back and apologize!" The next person would say the exact opposite. How was I supposed to figure out who I should be listening to?

About this time I heard a sermon from Jeff Henderson at Buckhead Church in Atlanta. In the sermon he talked about different life choices he had made, and while he was making them who and what he was listening to. Jeff passed up a big corporate job to be a pastor, but he was listening to God and to the mentors he had in his life, and that is why he is where he is today.

He told the story from the Bible about Rehoboam. After King Solomon (the son of David) died, his son Rehoboam was installed as the new king. But the nation of Israel was politically divided. King Solomon had taxed and exasperated the Israelites to build great cities and the temple in Jerusalem. The story in 1 Kings goes on:

> Rehoboam assembled Jeroboam and all the people. They said to Rehoboam, "Your father made life hard for us—worked our fingers to the bone. Give us a break; lighten up on us and we'll willingly serve you." "Give me three days to think it over, then come back," Rehoboam said. King Rehoboam talked it over with the elders who had advised his father when he was alive: "What's your counsel? How do you suggest that I answer the people?" They said, "If you will be a servant to this people, be considerate of their needs and respond with compassion, work things out with them, they'll end up doing anything for

you." But he rejected the counsel of the elders and asked the young men he'd grown up with who were now currying his favor, "What do you think? What should I say to these people who are saying, 'Give us a break from your father's harsh ways—lighten up on us'?" The young turks he'd grown up with said, "These people who complain, 'Your father was too hard on us; lighten up'—well, tell them this: 'My little finger is thicker than my father's waist. If you think life under my father was hard, you haven't seen the half of it. My father thrashed you with whips; I'll beat you bloody with chains!'" Three days later Jeroboam and the people showed up, just as Rehoboam had directed when he said, "Give me three days to think it over, then come back." The king's answer was harsh and rude. He spurned the counsel of the elders and went with the advice of the younger set, "If you think life under my father was hard, you haven't seen the half of it. My father thrashed you with whips; I'll beat you bloody with chains!" (1 Kings 12:3-14, The Message)

The upshot of the story is that most of the nation of Israel broke off and formed a new country. Rehoboam was left with only a small area to rule, and God's chosen nation was divided in two.

If only Rehoboam had listened to his wise advisors, instead of his foolish friends, he might have been able to keep the kingdom united. After all, his father King Solomon ruled over one of the most successful and wealthy nations ever to exist. Other kings and queens came to visit and were amazed at his kingdom and wealth. Instead, Rehoboam was king of only the tribes of Judah and Benjamin, and Jeroboam was ruling the other 10 tribes of Israel.

Jeff Henderson ended his sermon with these words: "Who and what you listen to is a preview of the future you!"

A light bulb went off in my head. I knew I needed to get a small group of people in my office who could offer me the best advice about dating. Then I needed to listen to them and not just to anyone's random opinion.

Chapter 6

Adam's Female Advisory Committee

After thinking it over, I came up with four ladies I wanted to listen to about dating.

First was Mariana. She was in her 30s, and was always asking me who I was dating. She had a high emotional intelligence,[1] and did a good job helping me understand how women thought. Her assistant, Justyne, would often join us in our conversations as well.

The lady who sat next to Mariana was Sue. She was a Steel Magnolia (a southern woman who is strong and independent, yet very feminine). She clearly knew how to dress and act like a graceful lady,

---

[1] Emotional intelligence (EI) or emotional quotient (EQ) is the ability of individuals to recognize their own and other people's emotions, to discriminate between different feelings and label them appropriately, and to use emotional information to guide thinking and behavior.

but, when needed, didn't have any problem cursing out some vendor on the phone.

As an added benefit, I was one of the few people who knew that Mariana and Sue had a big skirmish a long time ago and still didn't see eye to eye. I thought having people who didn't always think the same way on my team was a good idea. I don't want a bunch of "yes people" telling me what to do. I wanted a discussion of ideas to get me the best results possible.

The final piece of the puzzle was Bonnie. She was the oldest in the group and had been married for over 40 years. She often had flowers on her desk from her husband, and always seemed like she had a good marriage.

I didn't know of anyone who had ever assembled a team of people to help them with dating. Especially one with four women, ages 34 to 62. But in a world of many different opinions, they would be the voices to give me advice.

Mariana, Justyne, Sue, and Bonnie quickly became known as AFAC: Adam's Female Advisory Committee. Everybody thought that was funny, and a surprising number of people tried to get on the committee.

Chapter 7

The First Meeting

I still remember the first official AFAC meeting, I sent the members an Outlook Calendar invite. I had picked out a conference room, and even printed out notes of what I wanted and where I needed help.

The five of us sat around a table as I told them the following story about a girl.

I lived in western Kentucky until I was 9. All of my mom's side of the family still lives there. It is very rural, full of "salt of the earth" kinds of people. People there talk about Jesus on Sunday mornings, barbecue at lunch, and Kentucky basketball most of the rest of the time. (My earliest sports memory is Christian Laettner for Duke hitting the buzzer beater over Kentucky in the Final Four in 1992. Even today that game-winning shot is shown over and over again at tournament time.)

We moved away, but since we were coming back to Kentucky frequently, my parents bought a small condo on Lake Barkley. This gave us a place to stay so that we weren't imposing on family constantly. I spent a lot of time there during my summers in college.

During those summers, I was involved with a group of Christian students at the local university. They were very intense about their faith. Dating was frowned upon. I remember the first time I went on a lake trip with the group. I, like normal American guys, wore a swimsuit and when I got to the lake took my shirt off. I was quickly chastised and told to put my shirt back on. (Took me awhile to realize I was about to swim in the lake in the hot summer with my regular clothes on. Guys and girls were both wearing t-shirts and shorts.) However, for all the eccentricities that this group had, they really loved Christ and sought after Him. They led dozens of new students to the Lord every semester, and were really making a difference. That's what kept me coming back (not my desire to swim with my clothes on).

After my junior year I met a new incoming freshman girl, Jennifer, who joined this group. I quickly found out that her parents knew my parents when they were in college. My dad was a young professor at the time when Jennifer's parents had been students at the university.

I talked with Jennifer a few times when I was in town. She had her act together. She cared about the Lord. She was fun to be around. Basically, she was someone I wanted to spend more time with. The problem: she was now at the University of Kentucky in Lexington, and I was 382 miles away in Atlanta.

As I described my dilemma to my committee, I was encouraged: the AFAC members immediately had this situation figured out. There were a few minutes of discussion, and soon I was pulling my phone out and texting Jennifer word for word what they had written down for me to say. I remember at that point walking out of the conference room. They were saying, "It might take her some time to respond! Don't text her again until she does!" We were just outside the conference room door when my phone went "DING!" She had texted right back. We all looked at each other, smiled, and walked back into the conference room, and wrote another text.

Thanks to AFAC, after a few days of texting, I had a date set up with Jennifer for the next month, when I "happened to be coming through Lexington." Eventually AFAC let me carry the conversation more on my own, but the communication had started, and my dating life was now headed in the right direction.

Chapter 8

Look Like the Right Person

Once we had the date set up, the next question AFAC asked was, "What are you going to wear?" I suggested, "I have a light blue polo shirt with khaki shorts?" They liked that idea, but they wanted the shirt tucked in.

The ladies of AFAC then asked me what shoes I would wear. Little did I know how important the shoe question was to them. At this time I suggested that I have a pair of Birkenstocks I could wear. That was quickly shot down as "not going to happen." Sue bluntly said, "No Birkenstocks and no Chocos!" They took a laptop, went online, and found a pair of brown driving shoes that they liked. They then called all the retailers in the area to see if the ones they liked were in stock. Thankfully the $230 shoes they wanted me to buy were sold out, so I went to DSW and bought a similar but much cheaper pair that worked fine.

I can already hear the complaints now: "Adam, shouldn't people be interested in you for you and not what you look like? Don't judge a book by its cover, right?" If I could look inside and see someone's character and faith right away I would say you are exactly right, but as humans we cannot. When you first meet someone, 55% of your first impression will be "How does he or she look?"[1] 55%! Over half of what someone is going to think about you comes from how you look! Let me repeat that: Over half of what a girl, or guy, is going to think of you initially comes from how you look!

When I first started at Popeyes and realized I was the youngest person there, I knew I needed to dress well for people to respect me. Most guys dressed in business casual (nice khaki or dress pants, nice shirt with no tie). I wore a tie almost every day my first three years working there. I wanted people to look at me and see a competent man they wanted to work with. I remember after being there about a year, someone from a different department told me, "In five years you're going to be a CEO somewhere! Not here, but somewhere." Great! He liked what he saw—and he barely knew me.

Yes, the AFAC ladies were right on the money when they told me I needed to look the part.

---

1   http://www.forbes.com/2009/06/23/body-language-first-impression-forbes-woman-leadership-communication.html

It might look different for different groups of people, but dress appropriately for the crowd you will be with. I dress differently going into the business office than I do if I am going to sing and play a show somewhere.

If you are someone who really enjoys sweatpants and a t-shirt, my advice here is going to be difficult: Always try to be above the median dress level of the room. Ladies, if most of the girls are in cute dresses, at least wear a dress. Avoid yoga pants (unless it is yoga class).

Gentlemen, if most of the guys are in dress pants, don't wear jeans. All you are doing if you do not dress well is communicating that you are not worth as much as the other guys/girls in the room. You are worth just as much as they are! Dress like it!

Let me be clear here. I am saying for people to dress appropriately, guys and girls. Ladies, you want to catch a guy's attention because your overall look is beautiful, not because you look stacked in an inappropriate outfit. Dress appropriately!

Point to Remember:

Always dress as well as or better than the median dress level in the room.

Chapter 9

Act Like the Right Person

The next order of business for AFAC was making sure I was acting right. They went over every aspect of manners to make sure I didn't make a mistake.

Guys, you will never go wrong having good manners. Girls love that. Some things to do:

• Give her plenty of time when you ask her for the early dates. "Hey, pick you up in an hour" is not what she wants to hear. Give her a few days. This will give her time to think about what she is going to wear and to talk about it with her friends. All of that is good.

• Give her a general idea of what you are doing so she can dress appropriately. I have a friend who climbed Stone Mountain in high heels because some Schmo didn't let her in on the plan.

• Pick her up. Don't meet her somewhere. Pick her up. Unless you don't know each other and there is a safety concern, pick her up.

• Guys, be on time. If for some reason (traffic) you are running late, let her know.

• Open her car door for her.

• Open the restaurant/movie/church door for her. If there is a door, open it and let her walk through first.

• Pay for the date. Don't be a cheapskate. If you don't have much money, find cheaper places to go. (I am really aggressive with this one. It is easy to get in the "friend zone" if everyone is paying for their own tab. I don't want to be friends. I want to be more, so I am going to act like it and pay for the check.)

• If you are pushing through a crowd, the guy should go first and lead her through it.

• Say "please," "thank-you" and "you're welcome." If your mom told you to say it growing up, you should probably be saying it.

• If she has a coat, help her put it on.

• When the date is over, walk her to her door.

Those are simple, but if done correctly can really set you apart from the guys who do not do them. All of them convey to her that she has value. They also help everyone be at ease and prevent awkward situations.

Girls, here are some good ideas for you. Most of them I have had happen to me before.

• Be on time. I have waited for what seems like hours sitting on girls' living room couches while they are getting ready. I'm willing to concede 15 minutes; by 30 minutes I am already thinking how I will not ask this girl out again.

• At a restaurant, order something in line with what the guy is choosing. If he is ordering a $15 chicken parmesan, don't order the $42 lobster.

• Offer to pay for your part of the meal or activity. Hopefully the guy will step up and say, "Thanks, but I got it." But it means a lot that you had the courtesy to ask.

• After the guy pays, thank him for it. I get surprisingly irritated when I don't get a "Thank you!" after paying. I don't believe I have ever asked a girl out a second time who didn't say, "Thank you."

• If you had a good time, it is common now to text afterward saying something like, "Thanks, I had a great time. I really enjoyed the date!"

Here are some tips about how to act that aren't manners, but still you need to know and do:

• Do not cancel. It just makes you look bad. Believe me, it will get around. I have passed on girls before just because of how poorly they treated other people when canceling.

• Girls want to see confidence, but not arrogance. Do not be timid! I strongly believe the reason a "nice guy" will get passed over for an arrogant jerk is because the guy acts like a nice wuss. Don't be a wuss! I believe nice confident guys finish first. I get nervous on dates too, but I fake confidence. Fake confidence if you don't have it!

• Guys want to see confidence, too. Ladies, don't talk down about yourself or think less of yourself. He either asked or agreed to go on a date with you. He is interested and thinks you are valuable. Act like it.

• Be positive and optimistic. Even if you are a glass half-empty person, keep a positive attitude on these early dates. Very few people want to go out again with a whiner and a complainer. Also, this makes it easier if something goes wrong.

• If your date drops something or makes a mistake, be positive; make them feel at ease about it.

• Turn your phone off or put it on silent. Don't text. Don't take a call unless it is an emergency. No Facebook, Twitter, or Instagram. Stay off your phone!

• Do not talk about yourself the whole time. Do not talk the whole time. Do not talk the whole time. Did you hear me? Do not talk the whole time.

• Look your date in the eyes. Don't glare at them but have solid eye contact. I remember I was once telling a girl how much she meant to me and I was looking at my feet the whole time. She said, "Look at me and say those things to me! Don't look at your shoes!" I get nervous like everyone else.

• Say the person's name frequently. People love hearing their own name.

• Talk about what your date is interested in. Find what she is passionate about and she will probably talk your ear off, and have a great time doing it. If your date is talking, things are going well.

• LISTEN to what your date is saying. REMEMBER what your date is saying.

• Don't talk about things that are inappropriate on an early date.

• Don't gossip. You don't look better by putting other people down! You look better by showing you can keep yourself together and hold your tongue when needed.

• Don't talk about some terrible experience on your first date (i.e. abuse, divorce, death). Be honest, but avoid too much detail. Stay positive.

• Do not lie.

• Never put up with bad behavior. If someone is acting inappropriately tell them so, and leave if needed.

• Don't drink too much alcohol. (It also keeps the tabs much smaller.)

I've lived in Kentucky, Texas, Georgia and three different towns in Michigan. The stereotype that the South is all about manners and courtesy is true. The further south you go, the better the manners that are required. When I moved from Michigan to Atlanta, the change took some getting used to.

Point to Remember:

Act appropriately. Know and use good manners. Quality guys and girls know how to act appropriately.

Chapter 10

The Big Date

The weekend for my big date with Jennifer was finally here! I left work early on Friday, but before I left, the CMO (Chief Marketing Officer) came by to talk after hearing about AFAC and my date for the weekend. He, being a marketing guy, suggested bringing flowers when I picked her up. "Good idea!" I thought, and headed out (while thinking, "Wow, this thing has gotten big! The CMO of one of the biggest restaurant chains in America is commenting on my date").

Some moments in your life are almost surreal. Driving up I-75 to central Kentucky in my blue Nissan Versa hatchback was one of those for me. I had prayed about this girl for years. And I had for more than a month worked with the best dating team ever assembled, AFAC, to make this happen. This wasn't an ordinary weekend, with an ordinary date, with an ordinary girl. This girl was someone I could be in a serious relationship with for the rest of my life.

The drive to Lexington was six hours, and the sky was dark when I arrived. I swung by and picked up my Sprite Zero for the evening. (Everyone needs a nightcap.) I ironed my blue polo shirt with the hotel iron and was all set for my big date the next day.

I was supposed to pick Jennifer up at 2pm. I thought this would be good because if things were going well I could turn this into a marathon date. (Explained in the Introduction: Stacking several activities one after the other. This typically speeds up the relationship and, with the distance, I was going to need all the speeding up I could get.) In the morning I drove by her neighborhood, not close enough to give her any chance to see me, but I wanted to be sure that I knew where to go. Then I got a car wash and bought the flowers. Everything was prepared and ready. I grabbed a light lunch and then drove to her apartment.

I pulled up and walked to the door. Knock. Knock. Knock. The door opened, "Hey Adam, good to see you! Come on in." I walked into a very stereotypical 24-year-old female's apartment. Everything was very clean. The walls were covered in family pictures and flower paintings. And the biggest giveaway of all that there was very little male input in her life: a tiny tv. It was exactly like the Brad Paisley song *You Need a Man Around Here*. She showed me around and we small talked. After a few minutes she asked, "So what's the plan for today?" "I was thinking we could take a tour of the Henry Clay estate," I responded. (Henry Clay was a U.S. senator and even ran for president in the 1800s.) "That's in Lexington?" "Yep, just down the road." "Sounds good, let's go!"

While we were in the car (I opened the door for her) I noticed her fidgeting nervously with her purse strap. This was a great sign. She was nervous too! This wasn't some friend thing that she would quickly dismiss. This was a serious date.

We arrived at the Henry Clay estate, which looked like a large city park with an old mansion in the middle of it. I parked in the shade and we went in to get our tickets for a tour at 3pm. That was perfect, giving us a half hour to walk around the outside gardens and talk. She told me all about how she would be a bridesmaid in a wedding next month, how she went skydiving, and some about her family. She was talking quite a bit. Great! We were both getting more comfortable.

Tours, estates, and museums are great places for early dates. If you don't have something to talk about, look around and talk about what you are visiting, but if the conversation is flowing then keep it going. Tours are low pressure compared to coffee or dinner.

We arrived back at the estate about 3pm for the tour of the home. The guide was a younger lady, probably in her 30s, but everyone else on the tour was at least 55, and I would guess most were in their 70s or 80s. I'm thinking, "These people look old enough to remember Henry Clay! This could be a disaster!" But I looked over and Jennifer was excited to do this, so it was all good.

We walked through several of the rooms, and everything was impressive. The old furniture, pianos, and art were actually very interesting. Then it happened. Our tour group was standing in front of a large painting that contained an American flag that was touching the ground. One of the old geezers from the group asked, "Is this painting trying to make a statement with the flag touching the ground? (The American flag is never supposed to touch the ground.) Jennifer leaned over to me and said, "I was wondering that too." "Really!" I surprisingly responded. With a big smile on her face she shook her head "No." She had just teased me and was glowing ear to ear.

People often smile, but there is a difference between a simple smile, and when someone is glowing from the inside out. Guys, that is where you want your date to be.

Jennifer continued to glow for the rest of the tour. Afterwards, we got back in my car and I asked, "Would you like to grab an early dinner?" She said, "I'd like that."

We found a New Orleans-style restaurant down the street. That is where we started to get a bit deeper. She talked about her issues finding a good church, and

I talked about my job, and where I wanted to go. We were starting to get to know each other, who we are, and smiling all the way through. This was exactly what to shoot for on a first date.

The ride back to her place was more of the same. I walked her to her apartment door, she gave me a hug and said, "Have a safe trip home." I said, "Take care, I'll be in touch!"

That was it. Success.

Chapter 11

The Aftermath

I returned to my hotel room and spent the next hour texting AFAC and friends, letting them know the date went well. The responses came back fast and furious. Everyone wanted to know details. "What was she wearing?" "Where did you guys eat?" "How did you guys end things?"

When I returned to work on Monday, everyone wanted to know how my date went, and what were my next steps. I would tell them, "Hopefully, see her again soon!" I gave AFAC the full rundown of what happened. They all looked like proud parents watching their kid at a performance. It was "congratulations" all around. They had done an incredible job, and I had dated exactly who I wanted to.

A couple of days later, I shot her a text about something funny that happened on the date. She responded quickly, making me believe everything was good on her end as well. I was now ready to set up date number two.

Chapter 12

How to (Not) Shoot Someone Down

Everything was going perfectly. The date went well. I knew she had a good time. She was glowing! We had good communication after the date. So now I was ready to set up date number two.

I sat down and texted, "Hey, I was thinking about coming back to Lexington next month. Would you like to meet up again?"

Silence. I think to myself, "It's all right. She's just waiting to not look too anxious about things."

One day goes by and nothing.

Day two goes by and still no word from her. Now I am starting to get nervous.

Day three goes by and still nothing. "Is there something wrong with my phone? Did she not get my text?" Now I am second guessing myself and starting to get worried.

Day four goes by…nothing.

Day five goes by…nothing.

Day six goes by…nothing.

(I am thinking, "Come on! God created the world in six days. Can't this girl at least get herself together in seven?")

Day seven I am tired of waiting. I finally hear from a mutual friend, she isn't interested.

That was a big blow. I had spent many, many hours figuring out how to get a date. I drove six hours to Lexington to see her and six hours back. I planned a fun outing. I watched her have a good time. Yet, she didn't have the courtesy to text me, "No thank you, I don't think we are right for each other," or "I'm just too busy with school and work right now to date anybody!"

Although the ultimate result wasn't what I was hoping for, I was proud of myself. Sure, it didn't work out, but I knew what I wanted and went after it with everything I had. I sleep at night more easily knowing I had dated the girl I wanted to date and just didn't succeed. I would much rather have tried and failed than to have wondered for the rest of my life if she was the one.

Actually, I've been shot down before, and if it's handled poorly the sting lingers. I have made mistakes in this area, too, which leads me to ask, "What is the best way to turn down a date or end a relationship?"

I think the best way is to follow what Luke 6:31 says, "Do to others as you would have them do to you." If you were receiving a rejection, how would you want to be turned down?

The first and most important point is to always respond to someone who wants a date. I've heard some poor reasons for not wanting to go out, or to continue going out, but they were all better than no response at all.

Next, be kind but be honest. Don't tell more than you have to, but be honest about why you are not wanting to date them. I recently had a girl I had gone out with one time text me back after I asked her out again, "Thank you for the date, it was very thoughtful. I have really enjoyed our time together but I don't think we should be more than friends, so I hope we can do that." That response was positive. That response was kind. That response was honest. I can't be too upset. She said she had a good time, I did too, but it just wasn't going to work on her end. I remember talking to a guy friend about that and he said, "I love it when girls are just straightforward with me and shoot me down." At first I thought that was an odd comment, but then I pondered it, and it made sense. Shooting someone down in a kind and honest way shows respect to the person on the other end of the conversation.

I also believe how you communicate this rejection is important, whether that be text, phone call, or in person. Here are some rough guidelines:

- If just a date or two, nothing official yet, then text breakup is okay.

- If you have been officially a couple, then you need to pick up the phone and call.

- If you have told the person, "I love you!" then an in-person breakup is required.

Whichever way you are communicating, remember to be kind but also honest. Some examples would be, "I don't think we communicate well." "Spiritually, we are just a different places." "Emotionally, you need time to heal." "I have realized I need to get my finances in order before I can be a good provider." In order to be kind but honest, you need to be straightforward and clear about the problem, but not put down the person. That can be difficult, but if you think about what you want to say beforehand, you can come up with a good solution.

Point to Remember:

When ending a relationship, treat that person how you would want to be treated. Be kind but honest.

Chapter 13

I Was Dumped and Had Two Choices

I came into work the next day and emailed AFAC the news. They were so unhappy with Jennifer they even mentioned going up to Lexington and having a "talk" with her about how to treat people. I don't think those comments were ever serious, but I had people in my corner, and that felt good.

Unfortunately, I had to repeat the story many times as people wanted to know what had happened. Every time I went through the story, I had to relive the experience, and the rejected feeling was worse.

I was dumped, depressed, and demoralized. I didn't enjoy my job—the people in the office were great, but the work itself felt meaningless. I didn't want to be in the office anymore. I knew deep down that wasn't where I was supposed to be every day. I felt stuck, however, because at the time it was my only option.

Also, the previous year Dad was teaching in the fall in Michigan and my Mom had flown into Atlanta for a visit, nothing out of the ordinary (I thought). I will never forget, we were watching tv in my condo and Mom said, "Can you turn that off please?" and I knew something big was about to come out. My mind immediately raced to the worst scenarios: divorce… sickness…did someone die? Over the next 30 minutes Mom explained that she had received the diagnosis of breast cancer. The doctors caught it very early. It was still in stage zero. I did what all guys are taught to do in difficult emotional situations. I put on a strong face and prayed with her before she left.

Guys are taught from birth to avoid emotions; and if something bad is happening, we are told, "Stop crying and suck it up!" Basically, for any sporting event while I was growing up if someone was hurt you just put a band-aid on it and sent him back out to play and perform. No thought was ever given to how a guy felt. Any feeling or emotion can be perceived as weak by other guys, so we learn how to keep that deep down inside, and certainly don't let anyone see it.

I remember talking to Mom in the next few days and her remarking, "You are taking this well." The truth is, though, I wasn't. During the next months, I remember coming to her condo for lunch and just breaking down in my car as I pulled in the parking garage. I was thinking, "Is this going to be one of the last times I get to have lunch with my Mom? I don't think Dad and I are going to do well on our own." But I pulled myself together and put on a brave face, because that's what leaders do.

The truth is I was scared, and I was really angry with God. How could God let cancer happen to my Mom? When the opportunity came to be sleeping around with girls, I wasn't. When it would have been easy to get sloshed every weekend in college, I wasn't doing it. When the opportunity to cheat on tests in school came up, and no one would have found out, I didn't cheat. And in my job, I was giving my best, even though I believed the company was far from giving me its best. I thought, "I deserve better than this! My Mom deserves better than this! God, I've held up my end of this life…You aren't upholding your end!"

Soon after, I took a day off work and drove Mom and Dad to Piedmont Hospital, where Mom had outpatient surgery. Again, I put on the strong face. Everything went as well as it could.

For the next couple of months, every weekday, like a trooper, Mom got in her car and drove back down GA400 to the hospital to receive radiation treatments.

Basically, I didn't have the girl I wanted, my job was unfulfilling, and my Mom had cancer. I still believed that Christ died for me, but my faith in His goodness was shaken.

I remember one life-defining night, I was tired of it all. I didn't like the life I had. I walked down the street from my condo to a dive bar about a block away. The kind that reeks of cigarette smoke and serves food that tastes like it came out of a microwave. I walked there with every intention of drinking until it didn't hurt anymore. That way I wouldn't have to think about Jennifer, work, or my Mom's health. I sat there and looked around at the people who were there, and as unchristian as this thought was I thought, "I'm down, but not like this." They looked like they had been put through the ringer and hung up wet. Life was really hard on them. (The truth is Christ loves them and died for them just as He did for me.) Deep down I knew I was made for more than drinking my problems away. I had two choices. I could either sit on that bar stool and drink, or I could believe I was made for more. I could either give up, or I could plod forward.

I decided to plod back to my apartment sober that night. I didn't have great faith. I didn't even know if I believed that God was good. All I knew is I believed in Him and He let some terrible thing happen to my Mom. I went online and googled something like, "God is good." And somehow I got to a Youtube video from Gateway Church Worship with Kari Jobe singing, *You are Good.* It's a powerful song with these lyrics:

> Your kindness leads me to repentance
> Your goodness draws me to your side
> Your mercy calls me to be like You

Your favor is my delight
Everyday I'll awaken my praise
and pour out a song from my heart

You are good, You are good
You are good and Your mercy is forever
You are good, You are good
You are good, and Your mercy is forever

Your kindness leads me to repentance
Your goodness draws me to Your side
Your mercy calls me to be like You
Your favor is my delight
Everyday I'll awaken my praise
and pour out a song from my heart

Your kindness is forever
Your goodness is forever
Your mercy is forever, forever

You are good, You are good
You are good and Your mercy is forever
You are good, You are good
You are good, and Your mercy is forever[1]

Over the next few days and weeks I sat on my
living room floor and listened to that song over and
over. Not a lot changed in my circumstances, but

---

1   https://www.youtube.com/watch?v=Mol9SiX3jEY

slowly I was changing on the inside.   My angry, hardened heart was softening.

Point to Remember:

When you are dumped, you have two choices.   You can wallow and feel bad for yourself, or you can plod ahead.   Plodding ahead and moving forward is the only answer that will eventually make your pain and problems go away.

Chapter 14

What Next?

Real Estate

I started asking myself, "If I don't want to be where I am in life, where do I want to be?" I had always wanted to be an entrepreneur and own my own business. So I asked everyone I knew who owned a business to lunch. A couple of them were just out of my league. They were talking about investing $3 million here or there. I barely had three dollars to invest. Some just preached at me on how to act, or about some spiritual truth.

Finally, I had lunch with Darrell, who worked about 20 feet away from me at Popeyes. I knew he had worked in real estate before the financial collapse of 2008, and his wife was still running their business while he was working in the corporate world to help pay the bills during the downturn. Sitting at Moe's eating a burrito, he told me about how he had just bid $17,000 on a house. It was not on the best side of town, but the low amount got my attention. He told me, "Adam, do you want to own a business? Just come up with $17,000 and buy a house to rent out."

About six months later, after begging every bank in the city to give me an investor loan for a property (remember the 2008 financial crisis: getting a loan was very difficult during those times), I had the money for a real estate deal. Darrell's wife found a loan officer who thought outside the box and gave me a loan.

I soon bought a dump of a foreclosed townhome in Sandy Springs (northern suburb of Atlanta), and I was "in the game." It took me several months of working nights and weekends to get that house into shape so that someone could live in it. About 18 months after my original conversation with Darrell, I earned my first rent check. Then I bought a second foreclosure and remodeled it. Now my favorite day of the month is the first. Rent checks are due!

Music

Another item on my list of "Things I Want to Do" was sing. At the time I was friends with a graphic designer who put together the album covers for Chris Tomlin, Matt Redman, and all the Passion singers (they produce a lot of the Christian music that is on the radio). I asked my friend, "Where does Chris Tomlin go if he needs a voice lesson?" He told me, "We send all our people to Jan Smith Studios. David Crowder is taking lessons there now!" I went online and found the number for the studio. The receptionist answered the phone and told me the wait list was eight months, and they usually only work with professionals. I had to smooth talk my way through the professional part and she put my name on the list.

Sure enough, about eight months later I got a call from a guy named Peter Vogl. "Hey Adam, I teach lessons with Jan Smith and now have a time for you to come in and audition for a slot." So later that week I drove into the city with my cheap guitar that I bought in high school and went to audition. As, I walked in, I saw platinum records on the wall from every genre: Usher, Matchbox 20, Justin Bieber, The Band Perry, Shania Twain. The pictures and records on the wall went on and on. Peter came out and took me into his individual studio. It was clear from the start that I was one of the worst vocalists he was working with. He probably should have shown me the door. I had zero vocal training ever, but somehow he agreed to give me lessons.

Peter built me from the ground up. It took me a month to learn how to breathe correctly before I even sang a note. About the only good thing I had going for me was I didn't have any bad habits; in fact, I had no singing habits at all.

After a few months I started to write my first song. And guess what it was about? Jennifer. A girl from my hometown who never called me again. It wasn't the greatest song ever written, but it was a start.

Mom

Finally, and most important, after her treatment my Mom was cancer free (and still is!!!). Little by little my anger at God dissipated. I had to realize that God truly is good. Psalm 136:1 says, "Give thanks to the Lord, for he is good. His love endures forever."

It was important for me to reconcile God's goodness with the evil that happens in the world. At some point in our lives all Christians have to deal with that question. I think my friend Josh said it well, when I asked him why my Mom got cancer:

"God is in charge, but He's not always in control. He gave earth to man, man gave it over to the enemy through his fall (Genesis 3), and Jesus won it back for man. But at the moment that's only accessible through faith. So, though God is sovereignly working on some things, the world is still under the fallen system and man's delegated authority given over to Satan. That's why earth isn't heaven yet. Even though the sons of God, through faith, are bringing much heaven to earth and revealing the nature and goodness of God in the midst of destruction. So, as the church steps into her place of authority more and more, we see heaven invading earth more and more."

God didn't give my Mom cancer; living in a fallen world did that. God isn't causing the bad stuff that happens in the world. He is redeeming the bad stuff in the world through His Son and followers. God paid the price on the cross for my Mom's healing of cancer. "This is the kind of life you've been invited into, the kind of life Christ lived. He suffered everything that came his way so you would know that it could be done, and also know how to do it, step-by-step. He never did one thing wrong, not once said anything amiss. They called him every name in the book and he said nothing back. He suffered in silence, content to let God set things right. He used his servant body to carry our sins to the Cross so we could be rid of sin, free to live the right way. His wounds became your healing. You were lost sheep with no idea who you were or where you were going. Now you're named and kept for good by the Shepherd of your soul" (1 Peter 2:24-25, The Message).

Thankfully, Mom was cancer free. If anyone reading this is in need of a miracle for yourself or a family member, it is possible. Find a worship song like I did that helps bring you faith. Read the Bible. It is full of God's miraculous power, showing that He is taking care of His people. Find a church or friend who has big faith and get them to pray and agree with you. The 23rd Psalm says, "The Lord is my shepherd, I lack nothing."

You might disagree with where I came out on God's Sovereignty. No worries. Let's be friends anyway.

Point to Remember:

Often, a lot of good can come out of the tough times. Being really down helped me realize who I was. That is very important when dating someone. It gave me a strong desire to change my circumstances. It helped motivate me to become an entrepreneur and musician. After renovating two properties, I was making enough to go part time with my corporate job, thus freeing me to practice music (and write this book). When I was breaking up with Natalie (from Chapter 2), she said something that struck me, "You know who you are. I don't know who I am." The reason I deeply know who I am is because I chose to have faith that God was good, even when it didn't seem like it. I chose to believe God had good plans for me, even when circumstances looked like they were going poorly. If I hadn't been dumped by Jennifer, I would very likely not be accomplishing my hopes and dreams with the real estate and music. God was at work all along.

Sidenote:

Notice I wasn't dating much during this struggle. I was hung up on Jennifer (I did not put a period and move on—my advice in Chapter 2), and I was dealing with family issues. Very common advice in

Christian circles is, "Take a year off from dating!" I don't disagree with the idea of taking a break, but I don't think there is a recommended time period for emotional healing. This process of healing, and also learning who I was, took me about two years. At the beginning of this time I was undateable, but by the end I was finally whole again and ready to find someone. I believe a much better statement than, "I'm taking a year off from dating," is, "I'm not dating until I am whole enough to love someone as she deserves to be loved."

Chapter 15

Be the Right Person

I didn't realize at the time, but AFAC was turning me into the right person. I like how Andy Stanley says it, "Are you who the person of your dreams is looking for?"

People have in mind who they want to spend forever with. They could be attractive, honest, tall, dark, handsome, pretty, 6'1", nice, a leader, into music, into skating, into traveling, into sports, Republican, Democrat, clean, messy, a nice dresser. And if you are feeling holy that day you might put some faith characteristics in there like Christ-centered or servant-minded. Everyone has a list of attributes for the ideal partner. Fine, but are you who your ideal partner is looking for?

I love goals, and have a whiteboard in my living room where I write down my goals. Why? Because I like to know what I am shooting for. I think knowing what you are looking for with dating is good and positive. But most of us just look for the person with those qualities and attributes and never really ask the question, "Am I who the person of my dreams is looking for?"

I often see people looking for the right person online, looking for the right person at church, looking for the right person at work, looking for the right person at the mall, pretty much 24/7 chasing what in their mind is the right person. What if, instead of looking for the right person, you focused on being the right person?

Often what we want in another person doesn't match how we are behaving or acting. As a guy, I have more experience listening to guys talk about girls. Sometimes the guy is out of shape, has questionable character, and does not have a good job; and he is trying to get a particular girl who is fit, loves Jesus, and is successful. I will inevitably see that girl a couple of months later dating a well put together banker, who is in church regularly. And the first guy is still single.

Guys, if you want a physically fit, attractive lady, then get your butt to the gym and dress well. If a girl is attractive, she will want an attractive guy. Obviously, you don't want a gold digger for a partner (both guys and girls do it), but you need to be able to provide and be successful at what you do. I recently had a conversation with a girl who was complaining about the type of guys she was attracting. She said, "I'm looking for a guy who would be a good father, but all the guys are just interested in one thing. The wrong thing!" Then I looked through her Facebook pictures and understood why: "Hey, girl, put more clothes on!"

Point to Remember:

In order to find the right person, you need to be the right person.

Section 2
Study Questions

1. Who and what are you listening to about dating? Do you have a person or group of people who give you wise counsel? If you need dating help, who would be the best person for you to ask?

2. Do you dress as well as or better than the median dress level in the room?

3. Do you know and use good manners? What improvements can you make to show you value and respect the girl (or guy) you are dating?

4. How do you end relationships? Are you kind but honest?

5. If you've been dumped, are you wallowing and feeling bad for yourself, or are you plodding ahead?

6. Is your life to a point where you should be dating?

7. Are you the person who the person of your dreams is looking for? What changes should you make?

<u>Section Three</u>

Go Forth and Date

"Take time to deliberate, but when the time for

action has arrived, stop thinking and go in. "

Napoleon Bonaparte

Chapter 16

Get in the Right Environment

After college, I had moved to Atlanta and was searching for a church to attend. I looked online, found a list of churches, and checked out ones that looked appealing. I started off at one of the larger churches in the city with a group for singles who met on Wednesday nights. These young adults believed what I believed and were very passionate about their faith. Each week, I arrived early and hung around late to meet people. But I was having a problem connecting with the people I was meeting. No one ever asked me to lunch or to hang out. And no one really tried to reconnect with me again if I saw them the next week.

Most of the people I was meeting had a very different lifestyle from mine. We worked in different environments. We lived in different parts of town and usually ate at different restaurants. One day, when talking with the pastor who was leading the young adults service, I asked him to lunch. We had a friendly conversation and he recommended, "Just stick with it!" That's good advice.

Finally, after six weeks of attending on Wednesday nights, I met a guy who worked in a similar profession and we hit it off. I thought, "This is someone I could be friends with." After talking with him for about 20 minutes he said, "Actually, I usually don't attend church here. I just came with my friend James." I was disappointed, but my next question was a good one, "Well, where do you attend?" He gave me the name of another large church in town. (Typically the only churches that offer services, programs, and events for singles are larger churches.)

So I went home and looked up what services and programs this other church had, and found out they had a service for young people on Tuesday night. Great! I could check out this new church and not miss anything at the church I currently attended.

The next Tuesday night I arrived at the new church, and in the parking deck I saw a guy giving me the half wave. That's the wave of a guy who is not really sure if you are the person he thinks you are. Being new in town, I hadn't had anyone wave at me in a couple of months, so I waved back. I had no idea who the guy was, and at a distance he thought I was a different person. When I walked up to him he said, "Hey, I'm Jacob! I thought you were someone else." After that, I just followed him around. He introduced me to his good friend Blake, and I met several others as well. It was clear I was very similar to many of the people at this new church.

Blake planned for a group of us to go to the Atlanta Thrashers hockey game that weekend. (The Thrashers are now the Winnipeg Jets.) Attending a hockey game was perfect because I was the only one there who knew anything about hockey. We took the train to the game and had a big time.

I became a regular at the Tuesday night young adult group. There were five of us who soon became close friends: Jacob, Blake, Megan, Ashley, and me. When the weather warmed up we went to Blake's lake house in Alabama for a weekend of boating and jet skiing. There was a spider the girls wanted me to take care of, and instead of killing it, I threw it on Megan (I do not recommend repeating my actions here) and she screamed loudly. Everybody else thought that was hilarious. It was one of those stories that lives on long past the event, and gets funnier with time.

That summer we played on the same softball team, tubed down the Chattahoochee River, and had a great time together. During the tough times as well, like when Megan was downsized from her job, we all went to dinner to try to lift her spirits. Also, they helped me move (the true testament of friendship). We really built community with each other.

Toward the end of the summer I started spending a lot more time with Ashley. She was a modern southern belle: She always had a kind response and a classy answer. We dated for about eight months and then broke up. I don't think either of us had super strong feelings for each other. We liked each other, but we were probably not meant to go the distance together. And frankly, I had some growing up to do. But I have fond memories of our time together, and when I do talk with her, I always wish her the best.

Even though I didn't marry Ashley, the principle of finding the right environment with lots of possible partners is a good one. I met Ashley and built friendships and community with several other girls. I was in an environment where the pieces could be connected. But if I had stayed in my first church group, and never tried to find similar like-minded people, I never would have met Blake, Jacob, Megan, and especially Ashley.

Blake and Megan eventually got married. Ashley went to graduate school and spent several months in Seattle at Microsoft. Jacob left town and took a job in Dallas.

About two years after that original night when I was waving at Jacob in the parking deck, I realized everyone in my friend group had moved on, except for me. My community had evaporated. We were still friends, but Blake and Megan couldn't keep coming to the singles group once they married; and Jacob and Ashley left town. I remember one of my last conversations with Blake. He was comparing our group to the movie *Sandlot*, where the friends all come together for one magical summer, and then slowly move on. That had happened to our group, and I realized I would have to make new friends all over again.

(A note about my present day status: after almost ten years of being single in Atlanta, I am on my third different set of good friends. Nothing bad happened. We just drifted apart as our lives moved in different directions. Many of these people I see occasionally, but they are no longer the people I am living life with on a daily basis.)

A very common complaint among single people is, "I just can't meet anybody!" or "All the good ones are taken!" A few lucky people, like Dan, my roommate from college, found his mate early, but I and most others have not. We need to have a game plan because we can't expect God to drop Mr. or Ms. Perfect into our lives, in our timing, in our zip code, in our denomination, in our desired income level, and so on.

If nothing is going on for single people in your church, try a church that has singles programs. When I tried another church's Tuesday night singles group, it changed my whole community. Put yourself in a position to meet those people who share your values, goals, and ambitions.

Tip about Environment:

Put yourself out there in challenging environments. If you want to attract more girls to an event, find something they will want to do, and vice versa with guys. In one of my singles groups, several people regularly made references and jokes from the movie *Mean Girls*. That movie usually appeals to girls more than guys. Guys might laugh at the occasional Regina George reference, or something being "fetch," but for most guys the movie isn't enjoyable. But since our group continued to joke about that movie, I decided to host a movie night watching *Mean Girls*. I sent out the Facebook invite and almost every girl in the group came over, but only one other guy came. The two of us guys got a lot of attention.

The flip side of this is a couple of the girls in that same group were from the north and grew up watching hockey. The Stanley Cup Playoffs were on and they sent out weekly invites to watch the game at a sports bar. Guess what? Almost all the guys showed up and only a couple of the girls. The girls who did show up got a lot of attention. It didn't matter that the girls didn't know the difference between icing the puck and iced tea. They were there. Having a good time. While the girls who said, "I don't know anything about hockey" were sitting at home.

Point to Remember:

If you need more relationships and community, the first question to ask is, "Am I putting myself in the right environment to find the right relationships and community?"

Chapter 17

Get the Right Friends

I'm a finance guy. I think in terms of money a lot of the time. I'm not cheap, frugal, or greedy; I just naturally see the flow of money and how it works.

A few years back, I heard a minister say, "Take your three closest friends and what they earn and average it. That is what you earn!" I thought, "That is amazing," and tried it out. Sure enough, with me the results were almost exact. Three may not be a magic number, but take the people you are closest to and you will probably earn very close to what they do. If you earn significantly more or less, you would probably be living in a different neighborhood or apartment complex, eating at different restaurants, and taking different vacations. All of that would lead you to different friends, who would earn about what you do.

My first conclusion was, "I need to hang out with richer people!" Now I search out friends with good financial habits. I want to stay close to people who will encourage me to make sound financial decisions and help me get to where God wants me to be.

I believe the principle that the minister applied to income also applies to who you are dating. Look at your three closest friends. Who are they dating or married to? How do they date? Do they typically have healthy relationships, or are they usually crying with you on the phone? Are they with a different girl every weekend, or do they have deeper long- lasting relationships?

Now take a look at your dating past. Does it line up with how your closest friends of that time dated? My strong guess is that it does. In my early 20s, I hung out with guys who were not looking to settle down, and guess what, neither did I. If you had asked me, I would have said, "Yeah, I want to be in a committed relationship!" But I have spent much of my life with people who didn't help me get there. I hung out with guys who would rather play basketball on Friday night than find a group of girls to hang out with. There is nothing wrong with that, but I remained single, and that is not what I wanted.

Are your friends going in the same dating direction as you are? If you answer "Yes" to that, congratulations! Keep looking for quality friends to interact with, who will help you attract and be the best dater you can be. But, if your friends are not going in the direction you want to go, then it's time to ask some different people to lunch, join a new Bible study at church, or start hanging out with a new crowd.

I am not saying, "Drop your friends," but do understand how much time you are spending with people who aren't helping you accomplish your dream of being in a committed relationship. Some friends should only be in your life occasionally.

I recently met a friend for dinner, and he confessed, "I'm glad to be hanging out with you. Typically on the weekends I would just get trashed or go to a strip club." He knew he wasn't going in a good direction, and he was trying to change for the better. He was actively trying to change his friends and environment. He knew he was going to be alone as long as strippers and alcohol dominated his life. When he started turning his choices around, I noticed that he began to get higher quality dates. He was on a better path.

I have great memories with many of my guy friends, but now I want to move forward and be in a committed relationship. Proverbs 27:17 says, "As iron sharpens iron, so one person sharpens another." Find friends who are going to push you in the way you want to go!

Point to Remember:

The person you will date will be similar to whom your BFFs are dating.

Chapter 18

You Can't Do Everything

I was watching a late night game of bocce ball with my investment banker friend Chin when he said, "I am looking for a girl who can hang out with me for only about an hour a week, but when I tell a girl that, the conversation usually doesn't go well." I thought to myself, "At least he knows the reason he's single!" He lives in a nice part of town and drives a BMW. He eats at nice restaurants and is very entertaining to be around. On the surface he would be a great guy to date, but he is almost ALWAYS in the office. He often works 100+ hour weeks, which does not leave enough time for him to be in a serious relationship with anybody. I asked him what kind of relationships his co-workers had and he replied, "Lots of divorces and broken relationships." He enjoys his work, and is very good at it, but he knows he could never have a wife and family with that kind of schedule.

I remember when I was renovating properties, trying to play music professionally, and working a stressful full time job all at the same time. I couldn't date anybody during that period because I didn't have time for them. That was fine—at that time—because I was doing what had to be done, and was doing it only for a limited time.

You can see why my friend Chin struggled to find a positive relationship when he worked 100+ hour weeks, but a more common, harder to see problem is when you are overcommitted with too many activities.

I look at the schedules of many single people and am amazed at all they cram into their lives. They have all the freedom in the world: they are usually not bogged down by kids, or by family responsibilities, but they are still chronically overbooked. They will work a full time job, have a dog, exercise often, attend church often, serve at church, go to happy hour with co-workers, hang out with friends from college, hang out with friends from church, visit with parents, mentor kids, go on spring break to the beach, go on a ski trip, go on a small group girls' trip, attend early morning prayer group, go to football games, go to concerts, talk and text with friends on the phone regularly, and more. Everything on that list can be good and helpful, but doing too many of them at the same time makes life very stressful very fast. When do you have time to date? How do you fit someone special into your life?

I have dated girls with overpacked schedules, but every time, it has ended up the same. We have a lot of fun on early dates. Then when we need to spend more time together, I am pushed aside for some other commitment. The commitment isn't bad in itself (exercise, dog, friends, volunteering), but too much of any of these leaves no room for me, or any boyfriend.

How you spend your time is ultimately how you spend your life.

In 2009 a hospice nurse, Bronnie Ware, wrote an article called, *Regrets of the Dying*.[1] It went viral and was read by millions of people. She interviewed patients on the verge of death and asked them what regrets they had. She heard these dying people say two things over and over again.

First, "I wish I'd had the courage to live a life true to myself, not the life others expected of me." When these people realized that their lives were almost over, they regretted their unfulfilled dreams. "Most people," Ms. Ware discovered, "had not honoured even a half of their dreams and had to die knowing that it was due to choices they had made, or not made."

The second regret Ms. Ware heard most often was this: "I wish I didn't work so hard." According to Ware, "This came from every male patient that I nursed. They missed their children's youth and their partner's companionship. Women also spoke of this regret. But as most were from an older generation, many of the female patients had not been breadwinners. All of the

---

1   http://www.bronnieware.com/blog/regrets-of-the-dying

men I nursed deeply regretted spending so much of their lives on the treadmill of a work existence."

Ware's conclusion: "By simplifying your lifestyle and making conscious choices along the way, it is possible to not need the income that you think you do. And by creating more space in your life, you become happier and more open to new opportunities, ones more suited to your new lifestyle."

My conclusion: God gives each of us one life, and if we don't spend it on the things that actually matter, we will always regret it.

Don't get bogged down on the mundane tasks that don't matter in the end, while neglecting the dreams and the people that make life worth living. I realized three years ago that I had too much going on in my life. So I bought a whiteboard, I put it in my living room, and I wrote down the important projects, ideas, and habits I want to spend my time on. At the moment, there are six items on my board. (The first item is finish this book!) That way I constantly see what is important for me to be doing. If it's not on the board, it doesn't get my effort or attention.

It took some time to filter through the non-essential commitments, but I began only to say "yes" to the projects that were on my whiteboard. Then I had more space in my life, and was spending my days working on the important things. For example, I get asked regularly to lead something at church, but if it doesn't line up with one of the items on my board, I say, "No thanks. I don't have time in my life for that right now." I am passionate and feel called to work with single people in the church, so I volunteer with them regularly, but I often turn down opportunities to work with the children, greeting, parking, and other ministries at church. If I spent time working on all of those, I would never accomplish what I am called to accomplish.

You are not called to work in every area of the church. You are not called to be a workaholic. You are not called to be stressed out all the time. You are not called to be the friend who spends hours on the phone with anyone and everyone who is having challenges.

Here are a few items Christians are called to do:

Serve - "Each of you should use whatever gift you have received to serve others, as faithful stewards of God's grace in its various forms" (1 Peter 4:10).

Have Peace - "Take my yoke upon you and learn from me, for I am gentle and humble in heart, and you will find rest for your souls. For my yoke is easy and my burden is light" (Matthew 11:29-30).

Work - "The Lord God took the man and put him in the Garden of Eden to work it and take care of it" (Genesis 2:15).

Rest - "Remember the Sabbath day, to keep it holy. Six days you shall labor, and do all your work, but the seventh day is a Sabbath to the Lord your God" (Exodus 20:8-10).

How many of us rest one out of every seven days? No wonder so many of us are burned out. We are filling our lives with stuff that we aren't supposed to be doing, and often not accomplishing the things we should be doing. Currently, item number six on my whiteboard is "Sleep." I need to get more rest. I need to remember that God has told me to rest, and if I don't I am just hurting myself.

I don't want to get to the end of my life and have the regrets Bronnie Ware described. At the end of my life I want to be able to say, "I have lived a life true to God and true to myself. I have accomplished what I was put on Earth to do." I want to have a family with healthy relationships. In order to do that, I need to spend time on who and what is important in life. I need to spend my time with quality girls, quality friends, and quality relationships.

Chapter 19

Swing the Bat

It was Shark Week on the Discovery Channel. After coming home from work and being glued to the tv, I needed to get some dinner. I walked over to a taco restaurant near my condo and noticed one seat left at the bar, grabbed it, and asked for a menu. I was not there to mingle, just to eat my dinner and watch sports on the tv above my seat.

I didn't say a word to the girl next to me when suddenly she asked, "Will you watch my purse and phone while I go to the restroom?" That's not a request I usually get from total strangers—maybe I have an honest face. So I kept an eye on her purse and phone until she returned. When she got back she had missed the waiter to order, so I helped flag him down. I found out her name was Anne; she was very appreciative, and we started a conversation.

Anne was new to town—this was actually her first day of work. Then she asked me, "What do you do?" I said, "Well the last couple of years I bought houses, fixed them up, and leased them out. What I really like to do, though, is play music and sing." I pulled out my phone to show her a picture or two of my playing in different venues. This usually scored me big points. Girls loved that.

Sure enough, Anne responded, "Oh, that's cool." But then she added, "My brother played at the Tabernacle last weekend." The Tabernacle is a large concert venue in Atlanta that holds approximately 2,600 people. I was flabbergasted. I quickly pocketed my phone pictures of me playing to tiny audiences and asked, "Who is your brother?" She said, "You might not have heard of him, Kip Moore." I said, "Yes I know him. Plays *Somethin' 'Bout a Truck* and *Hey Pretty Girl*. Both had been chart-topping country songs, and he had just released his debut album. I said, "I actually played an early song of his, *Mary is the Marrying Kind*." She liked that. It showed that I clearly had a deeper knowledge of the situation. She explained how that song was his first major release with a big label, and it had flopped. The label gave him one more shot with *Somethin' 'Bout a Truck*. It skyrocketed to number one, which was wonderful she said, "because if that song had flopped the label was going to drop him."

We talked for another hour about her new apartment, the city, and her new job. As we were walking out of the restaurant, she said, "So you come here often?" Which is basically girl code for "I'd like to see you again, ask me for my number." I, like an idiot, said, "Yeah, quite a bit. Have a good one." And I walked off. After 10 steps down the sidewalk I realized how I had blown it. She was a girl I really enjoyed talking to, with phenomenal music connections, and I just let her walk away without even trying to connect again. The pitch came across the plate and I didn't even swing. I later looked for her online and with Facebook, but never found her.

Sometimes opportunity only lasts briefly and you have to take advantage of it. Even if she had shot me down I wouldn't be in any worse shape than I was. Don't be like me with Anne. Swing the bat.

Soon, I had another chance to swing the bat. It was almost Valentine's Day, and when you're single, that whole day can be a big reminder of how alone you are. I prayed, "God, I don't need the next Mrs. Folsom right now, but I do want a date on Valentine's Day." I was racking my brain trying to think of who I could ask but wasn't coming up with any good options (obviously not paying attention to Chapter 16: Get in the Right Environment).

I saw a girl in my building picking up a package at the same time I was. She was very pretty, and, as we rode the elevator back up to our condos, I saw that she lived on the floor above me. Then the next day, as I walked in my condo complex, she was outside walking a dog. So I struck up a conversation, "Is this your dog?" "Oh no," she said, "I'm just keeping her for a friend." I didn't know if she was dating someone, married, or just waiting for a guy like me to step into the scene. I noticed she wasn't wearing a wedding ring, but once again I just walked away without swinging the bat.

Then the next day she was out there again with the dog as I walked into the condo complex. This time she had a young girl with her. I thought to myself, "Well, at least I didn't make a fool of myself by asking out a girl who is married and has a kid." Since I had forgotten my clicker to get into the locked building, I asked if she would click me in. She agreed, and as we were walking to the door, I asked, "Is that your daughter?" She replied, "No, this is my niece. She loves the puppy." Once again I did not swing the bat. I had now seen this girl three times in a week. I didn't know anything about her or even which apartment she lived in. Remember, I prayed that I would have a date for Valentine's Day. But how can God help me if I refuse to swing the bat?

Finally, it was Valentine's Day. I did not have a date. I jumped in my truck and headed to a concert where a friend was playing that night. On my way out of the parking deck who was there? The girl who I had not asked out, not asked which apartment she was in, or anything about her life. Just like with Anne previously, I left. God had answered my prayer and provided. I didn't take advantage of it. She was alone on Valentine's Day, too. I believe she was my answer to prayer. I just never swung the bat.

Point to Remember:

Guys: If you are alone and looking for somebody, you have to be ready to ask. Don't worry about failure. Sometimes you are going to get shot down. It doesn't feel great at the time, but what feels worse is the regret of not asking.

Ladies: If you are a girl and looking, be sure to put yourself out there with lots of people and be engaging. We guys sometimes struggle to walk up to a girl and talk. A smile and a kind word go a long way.

Chapter 20

God's Way the Entire Way

Several months after my rough breakup with Natalie (the girl from Chapter 2), I met Rachel. We were part of a four week service group that was building a playground at a center in downtown Atlanta for women and their families who were trying to flee prostitution.

I was the leader of the service project, and there was always some albatross of a person who was requiring my attention. So I didn't get to know Rachel well, but she was very pretty, very impressive, and very available. The first week, she was moving to a different apartment and things weren't going well. The U-Haul reservation had been a mess, and she had to drive out of her way to pick it up, but she had the best attitude. Then, the next week, a friend had borrowed her car and wrecked it, causing damage to the front headlights. Despite the difficult circumstances, again, she had a great attitude.

When we were close to finishing the playground building project, I called Rachel and asked her out for the following week. She accepted! And in the meantime, I hadn't seen Natalie in months. What happened? Natalie sent me this email:

Hey Adam,

How are you doing? I hope all is well with you and your family. Do you think we could grab lunch or coffee sometime? I owe you an apology and I would like to do that in person if you are up for it. Let me know. No rush.

Natalie

I hadn't dated anyone in several months and now, all of a sudden, I am dealing with an old girlfriend and a potential new girlfriend.

First, Rachel and I went to Flip Burger. While we were eating, I asked her about her hobbies and what she does for fun (standard early date material) and she piped up about running and how much she likes to ride a bike (not the pleasant afternoon casual bike ride I like, but the funny skintight outfit on a super uncomfortable seat). This immediately took me back to my relationship with Natalie, who had chosen triathlons over me.

Now I was sitting across from a girl who had passions and desires similar to Natalie's. Insecurities started creeping in again. I casually asked a few more questions to clarify—sure enough, Rachel was a fairly serious distance athlete. I thought, "Two in a row. You know how to pick'em, Adam!"

Don't get me wrong, I like being healthy, and I want the girls I'm interested in to be healthy. But there is a big difference between going for an hour of exercise a few times a week and training for many hours every day. Will Rachel have time for me? Is this something she will want to do all her life? Since I was on a first date, I kept the conversation positive and casual, and we moved onto other topics. The date went great. Then we agreed to see each other the next week.

A couple of days later I had lunch with Natalie. Did she want to get back together, or just clear the air? I got to the restaurant first, and when she walked in she gave me a hug. Over lunch, she told me about her last few months (which were really tough) and she apologized for things she said and did. I got the feeling this lunch was more for her to put a period on our past relationship. That was fine with me.

The next week I was out with Rachel on date number two, but I still had the emotional upheaval of reliving some of the breakup with Natalie. Could I care for Rachel even though she, too, was a runner?

As we were talking I began to realize that she was poking around on some topics as well. She kept bringing the conversation back to arrogance, and people with big egos. I started to put the pieces together; she has some baggage as well. The last person she seriously dated had an enormous ego, and she was insecure that I would have that same issue. I thought, "She is having the same thoughts go through her head as I do in mine, just with different topics."

Rachel and I went out a few more times and then we hit a standstill. Basically, I was just trying to fake it through my insecurities, while she was letting hers paralyze her. One night she called me up and said, "Hey, can we talk a minute?" Then I heard the long list of things about why I'm "such a great guy," which was followed by the dreaded, "Let's just be friends for now."

I was frustrated, because I had tried hard to win her heart. I had taken her up to the top of a tall building with a blanket and we sat on the tailgate of my truck overlooking the city. I complimented her more than any other girl I had ever dated. I tried to be funny. I really listened when she talked. She was one of the few girls I had ever met who I could never get enough of. A few hours with Rachel felt like five minutes. She could handle my lifestyle of entrepreneur, musician, and part-time financial analyst. I could see coming home from a disappointing day and Rachel being so encouraging.

At the same time, I was also struggling with my house flipping, my music, and my finances. I was complaining to anyone who would listen. Would my baggage, or Rachel's baggage, really end our relationship before it started? How could we move forward?

A couple of days later I was on my way to LA Fitness to work out, really griping at God and giving Him a hard time for my troubles. But then it finally hit me (or God hit me). The problem was "I." I was the one stressed out at problems in the office. I was the one exhausted with my house flipping. I was the one impatient with my music career. And finally, I was the failure with Rachel.

Where was God in any of these areas of my life? Of course, I would pray about my day and tell God all my problems, just as most Christians do, but where was my reliance on God's faithfulness? Where was my release of situations, so God could work? Where was my confession about God being my provider? I wasn't praying to God, I was complaining at God, and then ignoring Him. I was trying to accomplish goals all in my own strength.

That week was one of the most humbling times of my life. I couldn't continue living life without God at the center. As a result, I began to confess before I started any task, meeting, or event, "God, here we are, You are doing this with me, or it's not getting done!"

And I meant it. I could no longer start tasks on my own, and then, when I ran out of my own strength, finally call out to God as a last resort. God and I will be together the entire way, start to finish.

With Rachel, I thought, "God, without you this isn't going to happen. Your grace is sufficient to heal both my hurts and Rachel's. God, Your will be done in this situation. I cannot see the future. You can. Lead both Rachel and me in the way we should go—either together or separately." Instead of my trying to run out and control the situation, I began letting God work in and through me. The God who holds the whole world in His hand. The God who parted the Red Sea. The God who is living and active in my life. The God who loves me unconditionally. The God who gave His only Son so that I can be in relationship with Him. The God of unending mercy. The God who has plans to prosper me and give me hope and a future. If this God is for me, who can be against me?

When I look at my problems and challenges through the prism of God being with me, I know I have nothing to worry about.

Sometimes I still have insecure feelings. But when I do, I immediately humble myself and say, "God, without you in this, it isn't going to work. I am no longer going to rely on my own strength." Some days I have to rely on this prayer a lot. But I believe it is the best way to get through life. God finds answers and outcomes we could never dream of. I think most veteran Christians understand this principle. Often we need to let God into our situation, and until we do, things can be painful.

The best way to deal with any problem is to start bringing God into your situation, and give Him time to work. If things are painful and confusing, hit the pause. I enjoyed a conversation with my Dad about this. "Adam, here you are an entrepreneur/musician/corporate finance person. Then you go out with a girl three times and you think she is going to be all in?! She has more sense than most. I believe in you. I've seen you take a house with nothing but problems and turn it into a financial machine, but she hasn't seen that." Basically Dad was saying, "Take your time. She will see who you really are and will like you, or move on."

Soon after I began relying on God instead of myself, I saw Him move in almost every area of my life. First, I was struggling to find a renter in one of my newly renovated properties. God provided a renter. Second, I wrote a song, *She's the Girl,* about my first date with Rachel. It was a giant leap forward in my songwriting, and gave me new attention from other singers. Third, God gave me another chance with Rachel.

The church we attended had a Christmas dance. I arrived fashionably late, and most of my friends were already on the dance floor. That included Rachel. She came right up to me and asked me about my week, and how I was doing. She was beside me most of the night. I also had my guy friends ready to be my wingmen for the evening.

The music was loud and there wasn't much talking, but my wingmen were doing what they could to make me look good in front of Rachel. With about 20 minutes left in the dance, there was a change in the songs from fast to slow. At that moment our group was in a circle on the dance floor and Rachel was across the circle from me. I took two steps out and froze. That is the moment when you realize the ramifications of what you are doing. This was a girl who recently told me, "I only want to be your friend." And I was about to ask her to dance. At that moment I felt a hand on my back. My wingman Felipe gave me a push (sometimes guys need one) and I walked to Rachel and we danced. Together. Just the two of us. We danced together for the rest of the night. I waited with her at the coat check and we sat on the shuttle together going back to our cars.

Later Felipe told me that when I pulled Rachel away from the group to dance, the girls in the group said, "Oh, don't they look cute together!" I might not have been the best dancer that night, but I had the only girl I wanted in that room smiling from ear to ear.

God was faithful. I just needed to invite Him into my situation.

Point to Remember:

There will be moments and problems in any relationship where the only way to get through is depending on God. He wants to help in every part of your relationship from the beginning. Let Him.

Chapter 21

Dance Your Girl

I was dating Rachel again when I learned she was taking traditional dance lessons. I probably have the tv show *Dancing with the Stars* to thank for this. Every Tuesday night for a month she was learning how to waltz or foxtrot, having a good time with a few of her girlfriends.

Her class consisted of about 20 women and 8 men. The men would rotate through the women so everyone got to dance. Most of the men doing the lessons were much older, which made me feel more relaxed about the whole situation.

At last Rachel's month of dancing was over, but now she and her friends wanted to take the Latin dance class on Thursdays. This made me think a little harder. The Latin dances have much more closeness and intimacy.

Rachel was not trying to cause a problem for us. She was just having a good time with her friends. But

I still didn't like her salsa dancing with a bunch of other guys.

So while pondering all of this, I was having dinner with several friends from church. One of the guys was Luis from Venezuela, and he liked to go out salsa dancing regularly. I asked him, "You dance salsa a lot. If you were dating someone would you be okay with her going out and dancing?" He looked at me, and without missing a beat in broken English said, "If you're not dancing, someone is going to dance your girl!"

He had laid it out for me in black and white: If Rachel wanted to dance, I needed to learn how to dance.

Soon after, I had the opportunity to take a salsa dancing class. I jumped at it. I was not the best dancer in the room, but I could hold my own. (The girls in the class said one guy smelled bad. At least I smelled good!) Now, I was ready for any dancing occasion. When I was on a date and they wanted to dance, I would do it.

If your partner goes to a wedding, or an evening out, and takes a spin or two on the dance floor, I don't think it's a big problem. You should have a trust level between the two of you that is high enough to know what is right and wrong. But dancing can be, and often is, intimate between two people. That should be taken seriously. I don't want anyone breaking the intimacy between me and who I am dating.

Points to Remember:

1. If you're not dancing, someone is going to dance your girl.

2. If your partner is really involved in any activity or cause, get involved in it too. You don't have to be passionate about it, but show your partner you care.

Chapter 22

You're in the Fairy Tale

After my rally in the past two weeks, with God helping me instead of my doing everything on my own, I was flying high. I even bought a Powerball ticket (but did not win). My relationship with Rachel was going well, and we were really enjoying our time together. She had almost no furniture in her apartment, so when she had me over to eat dinner, we sat on a blanket on the floor.

In the beginning of a relationship, gift giving can be tough. I didn't want to get a Christmas gift that was too big, but I wanted to show her how important she was to me. I came up with the idea, "I will make her a stocking to hang over the fireplace." So after googling and finding a local Michaels craft store, I decided what materials I needed for the stocking. I thought, "A needle, thread, and some fabric. What more could I need?"

I arrived at Michaels and was the only male in the store. Women were shopping with baskets full of craft supplies. I'm sure all of them wondered if I was lost. Why is a man in here? After wandering around, a nice older lady employee helped me find the fabric I was looking for: University of Southern Cal fleece. (Rachel went to school there for a year, and I'm a Notre Dame fan. So when Southern Cal thumped ND that fall in football, she was eager to tell me about it.) Once I got home, I spent the next four hours making a pattern, cutting out pieces of felt with her initials on them, and sewing the whole thing together. The finished product, I concluded, looked somewhat like a Christmas stocking. At least I had put a lot of effort, if not talent, into this gift.

Every Christmas I like to go to a Christmas concert, with a full symphony and plenty of old Christmas songs. So I bought Christmas concert tickets for Rachel and me to go to the Fox Theatre for a weekday show. I was planning on giving my gift to her that evening.

I was dressed in my navy blue suit, white shirt, and a red and black tie. When I arrived at her apartment, she was wearing a black dress, looking gorgeous. We decided that I'd drive her small Mazda instead of my big truck to dinner because of downtown traffic. (She didn't see me slip the gift under my driver's side car seat to save for after the show.)

Then came problems. As tends to happen in Atlanta, traffic made us late for our dinner reservation.

So when we got near the restaurant (next door to Fox Theatre), I saw Fox parking signs and pulled in. The person running the gate told me, "Sorry you can't park here, all the parking is prepaid and we are sold out. Please drive through the parking deck and through the exit in the back." I pulled through and realized there were dozens of parking spots in this deck unused. I looked over at Rachel, "We are late. Should we just park here?" "It's up to you," she responded. We didn't pay or have a parking pass. If caught, her car would be towed. But we were running late so I just parked in an out-of-the-way spot, and we headed to the restaurant. Once we got to the front, we waited until the gatekeeper was distracted by another car to sneak by so they wouldn't see us park illegally.

At the restaurant, which was packed with concertgoers, we were late for our reservation. And my gift was sitting in a car that might be towed at any moment. That would mean we would be taking a taxi home late tonight with no gift. Would this be one of those bad dates she talks about for the rest of her life? "I was once on a date with a guy who parked my car in the wrong spot and it was towed. We didn't eat, and I had no car for the next day!" Meanwhile, as we waited to be seated, Rachel looked over at me and said, "You're nervous about the car aren't you?" I nodded my head, "Yes." Thankfully, the restaurant seated us quickly, and we had a great meal.

We walked over to the theatre and found our seats. From that point on, the night was magical. The symphony and singers were wonderful. We were sitting in a historic theatre, decorated with lights, snowflakes, and Christmas backdrops. The ambiance was incredible. I was sitting, in my best suit, holding the hand of the most perfect girl I had ever met. Some moments in life are as good as it gets. That was one of them.

The concert ended and we strolled out with the crowd into the cool night air. The masses headed back to the parking decks to find their cars. I was just hoping we had a car to come back to! Thankfully, Rachel's car was still there. It wasn't towed. It wasn't even ticketed.

I turned the car on so the heater started as we waited for the parking deck to clear out. I reached under my seat and pulled out the gift that had been hiding there the entire evening. When I handed it to her, she was surprised and said, "How did you have this here?" I said, "Just open it." She carefully removed the silver wrapping paper and saw the stocking. "Where did you buy this?" She asked. "Umm, actually I made it," I responded. Now she had tears streaming down her cheeks. "How did you make this? When did you make this?" I responded, "I just wanted you to know how very special you are!" Which brought more tears. My effort, not my sewing ability, had blown her away.

Soon the parking deck cleared out, and we were able to leave. She was trying to hold herself together the entire way home. Every time she would look at the stocking she would tear up. In my head I'm thinking, "Wow, Adam, you really hit this one out of the park!" And we went home.

Points to Remember:

1. Great results can be achieved in imperfect situations. My Christmas date with Rachel was one of the best evenings of my life even though events didn't work out exactly as expected. Stop being frustrated with your dating, and enjoy the ride. Don't beat yourself up over not being perfect. Until we get to heaven, nothing will be.

2. You're in the fairy tale. We often fantasize about having a Nicholas Sparks kind of romance. If you've dated much, you've probably already had one. It might be as simple as walking around the block holding hands, sharing ice cream on a hot summer night, or dancing down the hall together when your favorite song comes on. The story above could easily be a cheesy made-for-TV Hallmark Channel movie. I was in the fairy tale that night.

Chapter 23

I Don't Know Why

Rachel went to visit her parents in Napa Valley shortly after our date at the Fox Theatre. While she was away I tried to text and call her regularly, but the responses were few and far between. We talked a couple of times, but it was more like polite chitchat around the water cooler at work than it was an early budding relationship. When I would text her about her day, and what she was doing, her responses were delayed and short. I was a bit worried, but I didn't think too much about it.

Rachel returned about a week later and I headed to the airport to pick her up. The pickup area outside of baggage claim was absolutely packed. It was going to take me at least 30 minutes to get up to the area where she was standing. She tried to come closer to me, but had so many packages from Christmas, that she couldn't move toward me. So I pulled around the line of traffic waiting to pick people up and forced my way through the traffic, one lane at a time to where she was waiting. She opened my truck door and said, "Wow, you just got right in there!" "I made it happen," I responded.

On the way home, she told me about her trip, about the creepy guy who followed her around the gym one day, and about how she hung out with her family. I told her about seeing my family as well. We got to her apartment, and the conversation got awkward. Neither of us quite knew what to say. I was still nervous from not getting much contact while she was out of town, and she was feeling that nervousness, too. Something started to be a little bit off in our relationship.

I saw her again later that week, but we were awkward again. I felt like she was pulling away from me and I didn't know how to stop it.

Soon after, I received a phone call from her, "Hey, I just don't think the timing is right." Whatever that means. Well, I'm pretty sure that means, "I don't want to date you anymore!" Then she said, "Every girl has a list of what she is looking for, and you check all the boxes on my list." "Great!" I respond, "So what's the problem?" "The timing isn't right." "Oh yeah, you mentioned that." The conversation went on for another 15 minutes. I couldn't get a clear answer about what the problem was. What had changed? Why had this relationship fallen apart?

I didn't know. I had a flashback to the first date when I took Rachel to Flip Burger. The night was cold, not good for a walk or sitting by the river. By the time we finished eating, it was too late to do much else. I was driving back to her apartment, trying to think of something to do to keep this date going. She opened the door and I saw an empty apartment living room. Her only furniture was a cabinet, a small table, and a bookcase. She had no couch, nowhere to sit.

At this point I owned two townhomes within a few miles of her apartment and they were unrented at the time. Usually, when one of my units is unrented, I put a chair in the unit so that I can sit to wait for a repairman or take a break when I'm doing renovations there.

So I told her, "Let's go get you a chair!" and she responded, "Okay, and your tire gauge light is on, we can get you some air!" So we drove to two different QT gas stations to find one with air we could use. Then I took her by my townhomes, both of which were almost ready to rent out. We grabbed a chair and ottoman from the first unit and put it in the back of my truck and took them to her apartment. Not exactly a first date that rings of the fun of a lifetime, but we were off to a good start.

Date two also went well. I took her up to the top of a parking deck in my truck. The night was cool so I pulled out a blanket and we sat on the tailgate of my truck, wrapped in a blanket, looking at a view of the city. We talked for a couple of hours. By the end of the evening she was glowing. On the ride home she didn't want to let go of my hand. And I didn't want her to want to let go.

Then my mind raced to the magical night at the Fox Theatre, and all the excitement and good times we had there.

Back to reality, that breakup phone call was painful. My mind and emotions were racing wildly to figure it all out.

I am a fixer. I fix houses and make them work again. I fix broken budgets, forecasts and spreadsheets in the office. I create and fix broken songs with music. It is hard for me to move on when I don't know what I did wrong. After a couple of days I realized that I will probably never know what happened, but I had to move on.

I drove by her apartment on my way to work almost every day. I often drove by the school where she worked. Every time I passed by I wrestled with my emotions. Was I a failure? Would I ever find someone as great as Rachel again? Did I say or do something wrong? Every time I would hear these questions I would have to tell my thoughts, "I put a period and move on! I'm not going to dwell on these negative thoughts and self doubt anymore!" (It's good to evaluate your actions, but to continually dwell on the negative is harmful, and doesn't help your future.)

Point to Remember:

Sometimes you will not know why a relationship ends. They don't always work out as we expect them to, and it's frustrating not knowing why, but it doesn't change the actions we need to take to move on from a broken relationship. We need to put a period on the relationship and move forward.

Chapter 24

Forgiveness Required

A few days later I got this text from Rachel, "Can you swing by between 5:30-6 and pick up your chair?" I responded, "That should work, see you then."

Over the last month I had written a song about our early date when we looked out over the city. (I had recently changed voice teachers. My old teacher Peter very selflessly suggested I switch and take lessons with a lady named Dionne Osborne. He had some health issues and believed she would get me where I wanted to go vocally.) The week before I had played my new song for Dionne, and I was surprised when she talked about getting a songwriting contract (basically letting someone famous sing it). That would be a huge step for me.

Since my entire time with Rachel had been positive, I wanted to sing to her the song I had just written about her. I would give her one last good memory of us when I came to pick up my chair.

When I arrived at her apartment we exchanged pleasantries and a hug. "I brought my guitar. I wanted to sing you that song that I've been telling you about." "Oh, a show. All right!" She seemed pleased.

We walked into her apartment and continued with some awkward small talk. I was hoping at some point that one of us would say something funny to make the awkward go away. I didn't want to dive right into singing or talking about how we were ending things. I wanted to end things positively, but I also wanted to make sure we were clear on where we stood and what we were doing.

I'd been in her apartment about two minutes and her phone rang. It was the gate, and she buzzed someone in. "That's strange, I wonder if that could be my Dad?" she said. This is rolling around in my head: "Am I about to meet her Dad for the first time as I am breaking up with her?" Back to awkward.

About a minute later there was a knock on her door. She opened it and a guy in a U.S. Marines shirt about my age came in. He walked right up to me and said, "Hey, I'm Trevor." I wondered, "What is going on here?" In an inquisitive tone I responded, "Hello, Trevor."

He walked over and handed her a blender, and they talked for a minute or two. I was still trying to take this all in: "Is she dating him? Who is this guy?

Why is he giving her a crappy used blender?" Finally, he came over and talked to me. I mentioned I was there to pick up my chair. He responded, "Hey, I'll help you take it out." He was trying to sound helpful, but was really just trying to get rid of me. I said with plenty of snark, "Yeah, you can take it out and put it in my red Tacoma outside!" He responded, "Let's take it together." And he grabbed the little ottoman that went with the chair. I picked up the big chair all by myself and carried it to the back of the truck.

As we were walking back in together, I realized that I needed a few minutes with Rachel alone and then I would leave them be. I tried to be respectful, and said, "Hey Trevor," and then I shook his hand, "I need 10 minutes with Rachel alone, and then I will be out of your hair." He responded, "I can't let you do that, man."

I was blown away. You're not even going to give me 10 minutes to talk with her? My blood was boiling. You're clearly trying to move in on my girl, and you're being a tool about it. We walked back into her apartment and we all had several seconds of uneasy silence. At this point I was really frustrated and said, "I'm outta here, this is ridiculous!" I picked up my guitar and as I was heading out the door, I said, "And by the way, this is the most awkward messed up last meeting I have ever had with someone!" At this point Rachel was chasing after me trying to calm things down. I was livid. Talking in the doorway I asked her, "Why is this guy being such a %&*^?" At that remark, he backed away. She responded, "He's being fine. I didn't even know he was coming." I asked, "Are you dating him?" I had almost totally lost it at this point.

Rachel was pulling me away and we walked to the truck. I again asked her, "Are you dating this guy?" "No no!" She responded. "That's Trevor, my friend from college. I've told you about him." (That was true, but I wasn't thinking straight at this point.) Then she said, "I'm not dating anyone right now. Believe me, it's either you or no one." I didn't know what to believe. We talked by the truck for about ten minutes. We got to a couple of the topics I had wanted to discuss with her. She assured me we were still friends. I had to leave for Bible study anyway (how ironic). I told her, "I got my ten minutes no matter what that %^&^^ said." "Be nice!" She responded. I hugged her goodbye, and she walked back toward her apartment when I yelled out in a humorous way, "And he's not invited to our wedding either!" She turned around and smiled.

I went to my Bible study and was still fuming. As I told some men in my group what just happened, Jeff, one of my good friends, put his hands over his face and said, "I can't take this. I feel so awkward and I wasn't even there." I had that sentiment again and again as I told my friends what happened over the next few days.

That first night after Bible study my parents were in town and I went by to talk with them. I explained the situation and how I felt. "I just wanted to go in there and pound his face in!" I had some terrible thoughts about what I wanted to do to that guy. I told them at one point I thought, "Maybe Dad can call some friends in D.C. and get him a one way ticket to Iraq!" Then I realized I was having the same thought as King David with Uriah the Hittite. My parents were obviously sympathetic to my cause, but were not overly thrilled with my being so angry. "I really think you should work on your anger and forgive. How'd that work out for King David?" Mom asked. Forgive? No way. I wanted Trevor to be accidently hit by a bus on his way home that night. No wait, "intentionally" hit by that bus! The driver would be performing a public service.

Meanwhile, I wondered, "Did Rachel know how bad I felt? Did she know how disrespectful that was to me?" Oh, how badly I wanted to send her an email just laying into her. I deserved way better than what I received that evening. I thought, "If I wrote a love song to some girls, they would want a ring right then and there, but you decide to bring another guy into the picture!" Thankfully, (this was the best thing I did) I knew to keep any feelings or negative thoughts at that point to myself. All that venting would cause more harm than good. I would look like an angry former boyfriend, and she would have thought she did the right thing by ending the relationship.

I was still so wound up the next day at work I could barely concentrate. I told one person my story, and then the whole office knew about it. Everyone had a comment (thankfully positive about me). I told the story several times that day. Every time I told it the fire inside me kept getting bigger.

At one point during the day I looked on my phone at the Bible verse of the day. It just happened to be:

> "But love your enemies, do good to them, and lend to them without expecting to get anything back. Then your reward will be great, and you will be children of the Most High, because he is kind to the ungrateful and wicked. Be merciful, just as your Father is merciful" (Luke 6:35-36 NIV).

I thought, "Well, that won't be happening today! I don't want to love or do good to Trevor. In fact I don't even care about a 'heavenly reward' right now. I'm not about to forgive him. If he were stranded on the side of the road, I would pass right on by. Just like the Levite, in the parable of the Good Samaritan."

The next day I was still angry at Rachel and Trevor. I had a lot of work to do in the office, which helped keep my mind off of things, but still I had no peace. I only felt anger, tension, and frustration.

On my way home from the office, I received a text from one of my co-leaders from the singles group at church. The three of us were going to get coffee that night at Starbucks. How odd, I am supposed to be a "Christian leader" of singles while having all this anger inside of me. Well, King David was a leader of God's holy chosen nation Israel and had the same feelings that I did, so at least I was in good company.

That night on my way to Starbucks, something started to happen. My heart began to soften. I wasn't listening to my usual country music. I had my radio on the Christian station. And the song *Better Than a Hallelujah*[1] came on. Some of the lyrics are:

> God loves the drunkard's cry
> The soldier's plea not to let him die
> Better than a Hallelujah sometimes

> The woman holding on for life
> The dying man giving up the fight
> Are better than a Hallelujah sometimes

> The tears of shame for what's been done
> The silence when the words won't come
> Are better than a Hallelujah sometimes

> We pour out our miseries
> God just hears a melody

---

1   In early 2011, *Better Than a Hallelujah* received a Grammy nomination for Best Gospel Song for songwriters Sarah Hart and Chapin Hartford.

Beautiful the mess we are
The honest cries of breaking hearts
Are better than a Hallelujah

That's not the usual song I enjoy listening to while racing down, or sitting on, the freeway (I do live in Atlanta). Basically, the song is about how God sometimes loves a sincere, honest prayer from the heart better than a churchy worship song. At that moment, I felt God was with me. He understood my pain and difficulties. They weren't anything new for Him. He was in full control.

Somehow, in that moment, I realized that this is one of the times in my life where I could truly be Christlike if I chose to. I still didn't want to forgive someone for something that was 100% (okay, maybe only 99%) their fault and incredibly painful to me, but I knew I had the opportunity.

Now, I better understood how Christ felt. He didn't deserve to be nailed to a cross. He was whipped 39 times for my sins, faults, and sickness. I was 100% responsible, and He chose to go through pain, suffering, and death to give me forgiveness. Now that I believe and am a Christ-follower, I have His righteousness and He took all my sin. I should be spiritually dead in my sins, but instead I am alive in Christ.

Just as my experience with Trevor was unfair to me, there was nothing fair about Christ's interaction with me either. I had sinned against Christ much worse than Trevor had sinned against me, and Christ forgave me anyway. I now knew I needed to go through that same forgiving process with Rachel and Trevor.

Points to Remember:

1. Don't get nasty after you have finished a relationship.

2. Don't send a negative e-mail, text, or message to someone once the relationship is over. It only makes you look petty.

3. There are often hurt feelings when a relationship ends. Especially if one person cheats, is disrespectful, or is just hurtful. At the end of the day, forgiving frees you from the person who hurt you.

4. Sometimes you need friends, parents, or other believers to rally around you when you have a big emotional issue. Don't be afraid to ask for help, and share what you are going through.

Chapter 25

Forgiving Ain't Easy

Even though I had a breakthrough, not everything inside of me was perfect. I woke up the next day and still had ill feelings about the situation. I had to tell myself, "I forgive Rachel and Trevor." Rachel was much easier to forgive than Trevor. I believe that when you really like and care for someone it is much easier to do what 1 Corinthians 13:5 says, "Keep no record of wrongs." But I was still hurting, and that hurt wanted to keep a record of wrongs.

I would occasionally daydream about playing hockey with Trevor on the other team. He would be carrying the puck down the ice and I would put my shoulder down and hit him into next week. In my mind it felt great. Then, I came back to reality and realized that was never going to happen. Also, I knew I didn't need to be dwelling on those thoughts. They felt good for the moment, but they weren't helping me move forward. So I would once again have to say, "I forgive Trevor."

Thus, I was learning to control my thoughts. If I just let my mind wander, I would begin reliving that awkward confrontation with Trevor. Instead, I had to focus on 2 Corinthians 10:5, "We are taking every thought captive to the obedience of Christ." We all have the ability to control what we focus on and think about. I was not going to let unforgiveness and anger continually run through my mind. Every time I would catch my mind wandering in that direction, I would say, "I forgive." And move on.

Little by little, thinking about positive things got easier. I wasn't hurting as much. I wasn't as angry. Forgiveness isn't always quick, but it is the only way to truly move past being hurt.

I also began to realize that anger was causing me to look at the situation incorrectly. Trevor had been a jerk, but Rachel was the one who needed to take control. It was her apartment. When Trevor refused to leave, she could have said at any time, "Hey Trevor, Adam and I need a few minutes." Then, all the hurt would have been avoided.

I often see others who have been treated unfairly be angry with the wrong person as well. They will be mad at their friend who told them about their cheating partner instead of being mad at their cheating partner. They will be mad at their girlfriend when they should be mad with their boss at work. They will be mad at their parents when they should be mad at their boyfriend who is treating them poorly.

When you choose to forgive, you will be able to move forward with less baggage. We all know people who have had tough relationships and never seem to be able to go forward. I am sympathetic about a failed relationship, but if it's been awhile, I don't want to hear about it anymore. You are wasting your life. Time to move on.

Point to Remember:

Forgiveness often is not a one time event. Forgiving someone may take time, but it is the only way to truly move forward from a bad situation.

Chapter 26

I Feel Forgotten

I was with my parents one evening, driving home from eating tacos, when I finally said, "I feel like God has forgotten me. I feel like He hasn't been faithful. Frankly, I'm just not that happy anymore." Dad responded, "I've noticed that you haven't been very happy lately." But neither of my parents were giving me much sympathy about my situation, or that God wasn't being faithful. My parents are more of the tell-you-what-you-don't-want-to-hear style rather than the sympathetic-let-us-hear-you-whine-about-it style. Whether they wanted to agree or not, I once again felt like things weren't working out, and that God had forgotten me.

My relationship with Rachel didn't work out. I had worked my tail off for four years, spending many late nights fixing up properties, and learning how to write and perform music. All the while I was working at least part-time in an often stressful corporate job just trying to hold everything together financially.

Most days were a grind: wake up, work hard, then go to sleep and repeat all over again.

I was tired. Tired physically. Tired emotionally. Tired of hearing from everyone who had a comment about my lifestyle. Tired of the people at work talking about my "days off" when I am not in the office, as though I just sit around and watch tv all day. Tired of going to events with extended family and having family members comment about how, "Adam's still single," or "Adam, do you have a job?" Tired of feeling like I don't fit in. Really, I was tired of asking, "God, have you forgotten me?"

About this time, the men's Bible study I was attending was studying the Life of Moses. The books of Exodus, Leviticus, Numbers, and Deuteronomy tell the story of how a man named Moses helped God's chosen people, the Israelites, escape slavery in Egypt. After leaving Egypt, the Israelites wandered around the desert for 40 years, and then finally made it to their homeland, Israel. As I was reading through the story week after week, I began to identify with the Israelites.

The Israelites were on their way to a "land flowing with milk and honey" (Exodus 33:3). I, too, was on my way to a new life as a successful entrepreneur and musician. The Israelites' path was often unclear. They had to depend on God to direct them. "By day the Lord went ahead of them in a pillar of cloud to guide them on their way and by night in a pillar of fire to give them light, so that they could travel by day or night" (Exodus 13:21). I have the Holy Spirit inside of me guiding me one day at a time (often I wish He would speak louder). The Israelites were learning how to be a nation. I was learning how to be the man God wanted me to be. The other similarity I noticed between myself and the Israelites: We both complained a lot.

While leaving Egypt, the Lord saved the Israelites in one of the best known Bible stories. The Egyptian army was chasing the Israelites, and they came to the Red Sea. "Moses raised his hand over the Red Sea, and the Lord caused a strong wind to blow from the east. The wind blew all night long. The sea split, and the wind made the ground dry. The Israelites went through the sea on dry land" (Exodus 14:21-22).

Once the Israelites were safely on the other shore, the Egyptian army tried to cross as well, but the Lord caused the waters of the Red Sea to drown the Egyptian army. "The Israelites saw the great power of the Lord when he defeated the Egyptians. So the people feared and respected the Lord, and they began to trust the Lord and his servant Moses" (Exodus 14:31).

I used to think that when God showed that kind of miracle, it would lead the people of Israel to never again complain or doubt God's goodness. But then I noticed that just three days later, the people complained to Moses that they didn't have any water to drink

(Exodus 15: 23-24). Just THREE DAYS LATER! I mean God just parted the Red Sea for you and you can't go three days without complaining!

Then I looked at my own life. I have never seen the waters parted, but I have seen God move and work. I was complaining to God about not getting breaks in life, but all the time He had been putting people and circumstances in my life for my benefit. God put Darrell, the real estate entrepreneur, 20 feet away from me at Popeyes. God put Peter and Dionne, my voice teachers, two of the best in the business, along my path. I hadn't had a full time job in two years, but God always provided financially. Before I was about to buy my first town home, which needed an enormous amount of work, God provided my friend Seth who said, "You can do this! I will help you." (And he did.) Every step of the way, God was there helping me, providing me with whom and what I needed.

Yet what was I doing all along the way? I was complaining. I was telling God how big the challenges were in front of me and how small God was to guide me through them. Any time events or circumstances weren't going exactly how I wanted them to, I was complaining, "Where are you, God?" I was like the Israelites in the desert.

Also, soon after the Israelites passed through the Red Sea, other nations began attacking them. In Exodus 17 the Amalekites fought against the Israelites, but the Lord caused the Israelites to win. "Then the Lord said to Moses, 'Write about this battle. Write these things in a book so that people will remember what happened here. And be sure to tell Joshua that I will completely destroy the Amalekites from the earth'" (Exodus 17:14).

The Lord wanted Moses to write down what happened, so that Moses and the Israelites would remember that God gave them the victory. God had been faithful to them in the past, and God would be faithful to them in the future.

This was a regular occurrence during the Old Testament stories. People would write down these stories and erect altars or monuments to remember what God had done.

So I went home to my computer and started a Word file titled, *God's Faithfulness to Adam*. Whenever I have a prayer answered, or a positive situation in my life, I write the date and what happened on this file. I read over what has happened in the past and remember God's goodness to me. And that helps me pray in faith for the future, instead of complaining about present circumstances. I can stand on God's promises, instead of what circumstances are telling me. God has been faithful to me in the past, and I want to keep a record of His goodness.

The Israelites did make it to their homeland. It is written in Joshua 25:45 (ERV), "The Lord kept every promise that he made to the Israelites. There were no promises that he failed to keep. Every promise came true." The Lord was faithful to the Israelites every step of the way.

The Lord has been, and will be, faithful to me every step of my way. Because of God's faithfulness to me in the past, I can trust his faithfulness to me in the future. Someday I hope to look back and say, "The Lord kept every promise that He made to me. There were no promises that He failed to keep. Every promise came true."

Points to Remember:

1. When you are discouraged about being single, or about circumstances in life not working out as expected, you need to remember God's faithfulness in the past.

2. Save a file on your computer, write in a notebook, or somehow keep track of specific times when God has been faithful to you. Rereading them will be a big encouragement to you when life doesn't make sense.

Chapter 27

The Recording

I was sitting in my voice teacher Dionne's studio one Wednesday night working on the song, *She's the Girl*. It was about one of my early dates with Rachel, what we did, and how I felt.

Dionne asked me, "Where were you thinking of having this song produced?" I had no idea. The only song I had recorded up to this point was a simple acoustic production. The producer who engineered that recording had since moved away. Dionne had worked with Drake, Chase Rice, and many other big artists, so I was open to anything she suggested. She said, "I send everybody to Jesse Owen Astin!" "Sounds good to me." I responded. (I later found out he had worked with Demi Lovato, Josiah Leming, Juliet Simms, Bonnie McKee, Cassadee Pope, Billy Ray Cyrus, and even Mott's for an applesauce commercial.)

Dionne talked with Jesse, and he called me a few days later, "So Dionne says you'd like to record a song. I have space the weekend of Valentine's Day;

would you be able to record then?" I was honored that he would even work with me. Any time he suggested, I would be there. "That works for me. See you then!"

A few weeks later, on Valentine's Day, I drove an hour to Jesse's home studio. I rang the doorbell and Jesse opened the door. He looked every bit the music producer: long hair, skinny jeans, and tattoos. We started talking and he was the nicest guy. He was intense about making good music, but never made me feel out of place or that I wasn't good enough. I was nervous, and new to the whole process, and he was exactly the right person to produce my song.

We started laying down track after track of instruments and vocals. The guy was a phenomenal musician. He played any instrument, but his special talent was production. He could put together 20 tracks of drums, guitars, bass, keyboards, percussion, synthesizer, and vocals and make them sound like they belong together. After a weekend of working together, Jesse made *She's the Girl* come to life.

I listened to the track over and over in my truck for the next few days. The recording still needed mastering and a few other items to be done to the song before it was released, but I was excited at what we had accomplished. I didn't feel great at the time, singing a song on Valentine's Day about a girl who had just left me, but this song was the start of my being taken seriously as an artist and songwriter.

Chapter 28

What Are the Odds?

Just a week after recording *She's the Girl*, I was running Saturday errands and went to a QT gas station. When I pulled up to the first vacant pump, I couldn't believe my eyes. Rachel, yes Rachel, was on the other side of the pump! "I cannot believe this!" I thought. "I haven't seen her in weeks, and now I randomly meet her here, right after I had recorded her song."

I hopped out of my truck and as I started the pump I said to her, "Hey! I've got something you should listen to." I grabbed the CD of the recording I had just completed the week before and handed it to her. "Listen to this!" I said with a smile.

She walked around to the driver's side of her car and got in to listen to the song. I looked in the passenger's side of her car and there were sacks of teaching supplies. (She was on her way to school to get ready for the next week.) So I just opened up the back seat and sat there. I'm thinking, "This is weird, but what else am I supposed to do?" So we were in her car—Rachel in the front seat, me in the back seat, and gas pumping into both of our vehicles. We briefly talked about our families, and then I said, "Put in the CD. It's about you." So we began to listen to the song about her, and how wonderful I thought she was. As the music played, she was holding back a floodgate of tears.

When it was over she said, "I've never had anyone write me a song before. How did you do that?" I explained about my producer, Jesse, and that we really worked well together. Rachel and I talked for a few more minutes, and I finally said, "I should probably be getting on my way." We got out and she gave me a big hug, and she hugged me like she meant it. I told her to keep the CD. We got back in our cars and drove off.

I had a mixture of emotions inside of me. I wondered, "Could this be a coincidence? What are the odds that just when I finished the song, at the exact moment I was going to get gas, Rachel was getting gas? What are the odds in a city of five million people we go to the same gas station? What are the odds that out of the gas station's 16 pumps, I pulled up to the one right next to her? What are the odds?"

Maybe there was something more going on. Maybe the God who created the universe and is all powerful, all knowing, and working out things for the good of those who love Him, is busily putting the exact pieces I need into place. Proverbs 16:9 says,

"In their hearts humans plan their course, but the Lord establishes their steps."

Point to Remember:

God is ALL powerful. He can cause any meeting, any coincidence, or any connection that is required. He never has limited options.

Chapter 29

And We're Back

Not long after our meeting at the gas station, I got a text from Rachel. "Hey Adam, would you like to meet for coffee on Friday?" I was intrigued, and waited a few hours to respond. I texted her back that I was available, and we worked out the details for Friday evening.

For the next couple of days I thought, "What is she going to say? Does she want to get back together? Apologize for the Trevor situation? Maybe she just wants to see how I'm doing and if we can be friends?"

Friday came and at lunchtime, before the evening meeting, I stopped at Zaxby's. I noticed near the candy machines by the door there was a coin-operated machine where (mostly kids) can buy temporary tattoos. As I looked at this machine, a wonderful plan came to my mind, "Rachel hasn't seen my arms for weeks. What if I put one of these temporary tattoos on, and tried to pass it off as if I really got a tattoo? That would really shock her! And it would be hilarious."

(For the record, I currently do not have any real tattoos, and I also don't have a problem with them on other people.) So I put my 50 cents into the machine and it dispensed a temporary tattoo of an eyeball with wings that was about three inches long and two inches wide. Perfect.

That evening, before we met, I decided to wear a long- sleeve shirt with the cuffs rolled back. I put the temporary tattoo on my forearm, so that when I stretched out my arm, the tattoo began to show beneath my sleeve. That was just what I wanted; I could barely control my laughter.

I arrived at the coffee shop a few minutes late, and Rachel was waiting, listening to the live music. (It was a guy with no arms or legs singing, and a film crew was there filming a documentary about him. It was impressive. He was not letting his lack of arms or legs stop him!) We found a table and she picked up two cups of tea for us.

She began the conversation: "First, I just want to thank you for the song. It's really special." I told her all about the behind the scenes, and how it was made. After a good amount of conversation on that, she said, "Also, I want to apologize for the night you came to pick up the chair. What I did was really disrespectful." As she was saying this, any anger or frustration I had felt just melted away.

Suddenly, I remembered my tattoo. So as I responded, I put my elbow on the table, with my shirt sleeve pulled down ever so slightly. She saw the tattoo. Her eyes almost popped out of her head. She couldn't say anything about it at the moment because I was responding to a very serious part of the conversation. I was holding myself together and not laughing. She was just staring at my arm. Then I decided to move my arm, and her eyes just followed wherever it went. Keep in mind I was still talking about my feelings, so she couldn't interrupt.

Finally, we got to a softer point in the conversation and I heard, "I have a question. What is on your arm?" I showed her my arm and said, "Oh, this is my tattoo. What do you think?" "It's very bright. It's very bright." That's all she could say. At this point I began laughing and couldn't hide it anymore. She then realized it was fake: "I thought you had gone totally Hollywood on me!" she said. Overall, with the conversation and the temporary tattoo, everything went as well as it could have.

I wanted to end the night with some fun, not just a serious conversation. So we went down the street to an arcade and played some games and had a good time. At the end of the evening I thought, "And we're back!"

We began to date again.

Point to Remember:

Forgiveness has benefits. Sometimes we are missing out on great people and events in life because we are blocking God's path and timing for us with unforgiveness.

Chapter 30

Listen and Sympathize

I am born a fixer. If you tell me a problem, you're probably going to hear my opinion on how to fix it. (You are reading my opinions on how to fix dating right now!)

I've never understood people who have problems in their lives, and then do nothing to correct them. My friend Chris has major health issues that can easily be corrected if he would eat healthier and exercise more. But year after year he lives in the same circumstances. Or my friend Mark, who has double the household income I have, but can never make ends meet. If he would spend less than is in his account, he would have more than enough to live well. But with him there is always more month than paycheck.

Year after year these people are in the same spot. I try to operate in a different way. If I am not eating well, or not exercising for a period of time, I feel it; then I go back to the gym again and things get back in line. I will occasionally run into a financial jam (everyone does); I just don't let it happen year after year. I had a big tax issue last year, but this year I have it solved. If something is a problem, I am laser-focused on fixing it.

As helpful as my fixing ways are in my own life, I believe they often hinder relationships. One summer in college I was in London with 10 other students from my school. We all became close during that month. One evening a few of us were sitting in my room and one of the girls was telling a story about a problem. I remember immediately thinking of a way to fix it. I shared with her one way out of the problem, expecting a "Thank you, that's good insight." (Oh, how naive I was.) Instead, she said, "Stop fixing, just listen!" And then she just kept going on with the story.

All through that month I would occasionally hear from her, "Stop fixing!" It took me a good while to put the pieces together (to most of the girls reading this, it is obvious); most of the time, people just want to be listened to and sympathized with. Those are not my strong points. I want to get to the point and fix the problem. It has taken me many years of getting this wrong to finally start learning how to do better.

After Rachel and I began dating again, I had a chance to apply what I was learning. Rachel and I went to Baconfest with several friends (a local fair with lots of bacon products). At the center of the fair was a competition table where teams would compete. The team names were typically ridiculous. We walked over when it was our turn to play, and one of our friends told them our team name was "It's Complicated" because they (pointing at Rachel and me) have a relationship that is complicated.

It was funny at first. We won a couple of rounds of the game, and then the referee pulled out a bullhorn and announced to the hundreds of people at the fair, "Team 'It's Complicated' has won three in a row! They are called 'It's Complicated' because of these two's relationship [pointing to Rachel and me]." That just changed it from a funny joke between a few friends to her being embarrassed in front of a lot of people. Rachel turned to me and said, "The whole fair knows, Adam! The whole fair!" (Whenever she was irritated she repeated things twice.) I understood that loud and clear, and now, being wiser than I was in the past with girls, I LISTENED and SYMPATHIZED. I put my arm around her and didn't say much. Amazingly, I was solving the problem doing almost nothing.

At that moment, I thought, "Am I a genius? Have I finally cracked the code and learned how to listen and sympathize with women? Does talking less really mean more?" Basically, hugging and keeping my mouth shut got the job done.

However, if the magnitude or consequences of a problem are large, then I must step in right away and try to fix it. But with something small (most problems in life are small), or if someone is just telling me about her day, I now try to keep my mouth shut and listen. If I do open my mouth I am sure my words are sympathetic.

This advice isn't just for guys listening to girls either. We guys also like to be listened to. I remember dating one girl who immediately started telling me about her day whenever I called her—and it would go on for a long time. Once, while we were talking on the phone, I realized I hadn't said a word for 12 minutes! Why was I even on the other end?

With the next girl I dated, every time we talked on the phone she would ask, "How was your day?" During every phone call, that was always her first question. I really appreciated that. (I have to watch not talking too much as well.)

Point to Remember:

Be sure with whomever you are dating that instead of fixing the little things, LISTEN and SYMPATHIZE. Everyone needs to be listened to and cared about.

Chapter 31

Joy

I don't want to pass over this time with Rachel too quickly. I have talked a lot about problems in relationships, but the flip side is the joy that makes relationships important and even necessary in our lives.

When a relationship is going well, five hours can feel like fifteen minutes. Whenever Rachel and I were together, I never wanted to leave. I never wanted nights to end.

When I was not dating, I ate almost every meal out by myself. Dating Rachel, it was nice not to ask, "Am I going to be alone tonight eating dinner?" She was there cooking or eating out with me. (I can also see why married men on average live longer than single men. She would want to make salmon together and eat fruit. My usual diet of burgers and BBQ changed and became much healthier.)

I knew she was enjoying the relationship, too. She had a difficult work environment and was often struggling with what to do. I didn't know much about being a teacher, but I was there to listen. I would hear about her favorite students, and what they were doing or working on. Her teaching was an important piece of her life, and she was gifted at helping kids learn.

Similarly, I received a call from her one afternoon, and she was crying on the other end. She had traveled hours to see her parents that day, and then events didn't go well. While she was upset, and looking at a long drive back home, I reassured and comforted her as best I could. I felt good that she would choose to call me. When you're upset who do you call? The person you trust the most to help. We were helping each other through life's problems, which made them easier to face.

One evening we picked up some subs from Publix and had a picnic next to the river. We started talking about events that shaped us. She told me about her best friend drowning in college and how that totally changed her life. Understandably, that had affected her greatly, and she was sharing it openly with me. She was trusting me with some of her innermost thoughts, and we both came closer together.

Not every conversation was deep. Often we just had a good time. I'll never forget sitting there one night watching the March Madness basketball tournament, when she said, "Let me make dinner for you!" So she went in the kitchen and started making fajitas. I was sitting there thinking, "Is this a test? Should I be in there helping?" So I asked, and she insisted that I just sit and watch the game. Now I thought, "This is as good as life gets. I'm watching an amazing basketball game while a beautiful girl is cooking me dinner." (After telling this story to my guy friends all I got was, "You are the luckiest....")

We were also progressing spiritually during this time. We would occasionally pray out loud together. (Sunday mornings were tough for us to be together because of different volunteering events at different services.) I remember we attended a worship service at one of the local theaters, took communion, and worshiped God together.

After a couple of months of dating, she left town for a few days on a trip to the Bahamas (her friend won the free trip with work). She didn't have much access to cell phone service or internet during that time. When she came back, she said, "I thought about you the whole time." Then she looked me straight in the eyes and said, "I love you." Wow! I was not ready for that. I spent the next few days thinking through all the ramifications of a girl loving me. This wasn't some casual comment or feeling, this was deep down I want to be with you for a long time, "I love you."

Rachel's statement was a challenge to me. I had poured my life and time into my properties and music. If needed, would I be able to put Rachel above those? I thought about my music career. Would I be able to put her above a big break or opportunity? Can I see myself with this person for the rest of my life? Can I financially support her? I thought about the high calling God gave husbands: "Husbands, love your wives, just as Christ loved the church and gave himself up for her" (Ephesians 5:25). Could I care for Rachel's life more than my own? (This works both ways once a relationship goes from newly dating to serious: guys must care more for the girls than themselves, and the girls must care more for the guys.)

A few days later, after really thinking about our relationship, I saw Rachel and told her, "I've really been feeling the weight of what you told me a few days ago. I love you, too."

We had a lot of joy, with occasional problems mixed in. But life was much better with Rachel there.

Points to Remember:

1. There is a lot of joy in a positive relationship. Even God said when there was only one human being on the earth, "It is not good for man to be alone" (Gen 2:18).

2. It is good to understand the gravity of beginning a serious relationship with somebody.

Chapter 32

Wrong Time To Fight

Sitting in the kitchen one day, Rachel asked me, "So hypothetically, if Sandra is in town, would you want to meet her?" Sandra isn't Rachel's actual mom, but she was an important mentor in her life. Rachel then went on, "To me this is sacred; I've only brought home one other guy for my family to meet!" "Yeah, that sounds good," I responded. All the while thinking, "Why is this sacred? My parents have met all kinds of girls along the way." So then I asked, "Hypothetically, would you want to meet my parents?" She agreed.

Fast forward two weeks and Sandra was coming to town with her family. We were going to have dinner at a restaurant Wednesday night. Then Thursday night Rachel was coming to dinner at my parents' house. Mom was cooking her special beef dish. Then we were planning to play a card game, which helps break the ice and shows my parents how this girl thinks.

The weekend before these outings were supposed to take place, Rachel was out of town. I understood that we wouldn't talk as much, and that she was often disconnected when gone. I might get a text or two each day and that was it.

Originally, she was planning on driving back into town on Monday, but then that turned into Tuesday. I hadn't heard much from her, and realized that we needed to get some details squared away for these dinners coming up the next few days. So I shot her a note to give me a call when she could. A couple of hours later all I got was a text, "I'm headed to lunch." At that point, I felt like I was not a priority; when I needed to communicate with her she was unresponsive. So I was irritated—probably shouldn't have been but I was. I responded with a very snarky text: "I would say something more but it will probably take you 7 hours to respond to this text!" Sure enough I didn't hear from her for 8 hours (I was one off).

In the meantime, the people she was staying with were having an emergency and she texted me about the situation. "Why can this girl not pick up the phone and give me a call?" was all I was thinking. Anyway, we texted back and forth a bit, arguing about things, and then we were both irritated.

The next day I got a call from her, telling me how hurt she was by the situation. How I should have been there for her. (I would have gladly been there but there was no way for me to know, other than a couple of cryptic texts, how things were going.) We were on the phone for about an hour after I had apologized for what felt like the 300th time, when she canceled both dinners and told me she would call me tomorrow.

She called the next day and ended the relationship. Yes, I was snarky, and even rude at times. I shouldn't have been, and it cost me my relationship with her. I hoped she would be mad for a couple of days and get over it, but I was wrong. It was over—and I was devastated.

I still don't understand everything that happened with Rachel. We were in a serious relationship, and all I could think of was, "How could this end over such a small issue?" I was so frustrated. I was 30 years old and had only found one or two girls who I thought I could spend my life with. It didn't seem right or fair to me the way it ended. There were days I told myself, "I'm going to be okay." There were other days I was angry. In the end, I realized I needed to learn as much as I could and move on.

There is only one lesson to be gleaned from my breakup with Rachel. And it is not:

a) I was wrong some.
b) She was wrong some.
c) I was probably wrong more.
d) I should have been more supportive.

Those answers may all have some truth in them, but they are not going to help me (or you) in the future.

There will be times in the future where both I and the person I am dating are irritated and say things we shouldn't. That is just a part of being in relationships.

The lesson here is to avoid arguments when the relationship is in transition, or before a big event. The timing of arguments is important. Sometimes you just have to bury irritation inside of you for a time and put on a good face. I was trying to fight a battle at the wrong time. I should have kept quiet, and then when the family meetings were over, I could have sat down with her and talked more about our level of communication. Our relationship was transitioning from getting to know each other and care about each other to very serious. Instead, it transitioned the other way, from going somewhere to ending.

The same principle holds true for holidays, birthdays, and any special occasion. If Valentine's Day is coming up, don't have a big argument.

It's a simple principle. If I'm about to get a promotion at work, I don't get in a big argument with my boss. In the same way, I was about to have my relationship promoted. Instead, after my argument, I was demoted.

Point to Remember:

Don't get in any big arguments when your relationship is in transition, or before any big events.

Chapter 33

She Made Me Better

Yes, I was shocked that our relationship was over. I was disappointed. I was hurting. But I was so grateful for my time with Rachel. I would have done it again in a heartbeat.

Why? Because Rachel put the best into me and got the best out of me. I recently heard from a friend who was visiting her mother say, "She always knows how to whip me into shape." Growing up, parents are supposed to be those people (I'm thankful mine were). Early in my life, they also took the form of teachers, coaches, and pastors. These are people who pour everything they can into you, and believe you can do anything you put your mind to. They aren't necessarily yelling at you to get something done for their sakes, but because they believe you can do something amazing with your life. Their love and effort causes us to aspire to make them proud.

I didn't realize until I met Rachel that a girl would do that to me, too. It wasn't immediate, but after several weeks and months of getting to know her, I was changed. She didn't push any of the changes, but deep down I had a desire to be…better.

I remember at work one day, in my spare time, googling, "How to be a better leader." That would have never happened before Rachel. I would have been more interested in trying to figure out who the Detroit Lions were going to draft next spring, or what traffic was going to be like on my way home.

Suddenly, I found myself really looking at my finances. For the past three years I had been basically living at my parents' place, while buying properties, fixing them up, and leasing them out. There were many months I was stretched thin financially (ever have a home remodel project come in under budget? No!).

Rachel was the most supportive girl I had ever met about my career. Never a complaint, always plenty of encouragement. I knew I needed to make the real estate business more stable, and find a proper home. I'm very proud of the unconventional career choices I have made so far, but because of Rachel, I was wanting to invest in something more than having a bigger pile of stuff.

Guys, feel free to skip this paragraph, because this is as sappy as I get. The truth is Rachel made me feel at peace no matter what was going on in my life or in the world. With her by my side I was fulfilled. Where most of what I had known before was stress from work, stress from remodeling townhomes, stress from finances, stress because Notre Dame lost a big football game…again, stress from Mom telling me she doesn't have any grandchildren! Rachel didn't complicate my life, she made it easier. I slept well…while dreaming of her almost every night.

Most of the people I had dated didn't make me aspire to be a better person. Most of them slowed me down. I remember a few years earlier a friend of mine, Jordan, who was just married, told me "Someday you'll meet someone who doesn't take away from your life, but enables you to accomplish more!" I remember thinking at the time, "Yeah that's easier for someone with a steady job" (and at least in my mind an easier life). Is someone really going to be able to embrace my risky life choices, support them, and help me accomplish my dreams? When most girls ask what I do, and I tell them, all they hear is, "Risky! Might not get a Lexus in the suburbs with 2.5 kids." But Rachel, unlike other girls, helped me accomplish more.

For example, when we were dating, I finally rented out a house I had spent months renovating. The next day I found a card on my door with this written on it:

Adam,

You deserve every good thing that comes your way. Congratulations on signing the lease at your townhouse. I'm so proud of all your efforts and dedication. It's inspiring to see you put 100% into all that you do. Never forget how amazing you are—and how much I believe in you.

Love, Rachel

With encouragement and belief in me like that, how can I fail?

I can remember how I felt in the second chapter of this book after a breakup with a previous girlfriend, and my feelings this time were different. In that case I was much worse off for being in that relationship. It didn't improve my life; it made me worse. I was a shell of my former self, unable to eat or even sleep well. When a relationship ends, you can see if the other person moved you forward in life, or held you back.

I can't be mad at or disappointed with Rachel because I was a better person for having been with her. I'm not a morning prayer person, but soon after we broke up, I woke up, got on my knees by my bed, and said, "Lord, I pray for Rachel...." I prayed that she would have wisdom and guidance for her day. I prayed that the right people would be in her life and the wrong people would get out of her life. I prayed for her work and family. I prayed for her health and living situation. I prayed for her even though I had absolutely nothing to gain personally.

Prayer was the only thing I could do for her then. I woke up the next day and did the same thing. I prayed for Rachel. After a couple of weeks, I began to learn and realize that this is how a person should pray for his or her partner every day. I hadn't been doing that. I'm sure many people in relationships rarely pray for their partners, and then wonder why God isn't helping in their situations. Matthew 7:7 says, "Ask, and it will be given to you seek, and you will find; knock, and it will be opened to you." We all need to be on our knees regularly praying for the important people in our lives.

Points to Remember:

1. When dating, look for someone who inspires you and makes you better. If you are going to spend the rest of your life with someone, make it someone who inspires you. There are lots of people to date who will suck the life out of you. You are better than that; pick a winner who makes you better.

2. God wants us to be on our knees praying for our significant others. If they truly are the most important people in our lives, we need to make sure they are guided and protected by God.

Section 3
Study Questions

1. Are you putting yourself in the right environment to find the right relationships and community?

2. What kind of people do your best friends date? Are your friends' dating relationships healthy? Do you need to spend more time with friends who have positive dating relationships?

3. Is your schedule overpacked? Do your activities move you toward your goals—in dating and in life? What activities do you need to spend less time on, or eliminate? What do you need to spend more time doing?

4. Do you need to forgive someone you dated?

5. How do you remember God's faithfulness to you? Do you need to start a journal, save a list on your phone, or start a file on your computer?

Section Four

The New Game Plan For Dating: Levels

"By failing to prepare,

you are preparing to fail."

Benjamin Franklin

Chapter 34

Commitment

I was sitting at an outside table at Ippolito's, an Italian restaurant, across from my friend Matt when he said, "Basically, Rachel just wasn't committed to you!" I was still trying to wrap my head around why Rachel had just ended our relationship...for the third time.

He put his hands out and then interlocked his fingers, "You're never going to find someone who is a perfect fit like this. They just don't exist, but you can be committed to becoming the person she wants you to be, and she can be committed to be the person you want her to be. Eventually, you will end up closer and closer to the perfect fit." (Matt is an industrial engineer and has a system for everything.)

I didn't realize this at the time, but when he was seriously dating a girl, he had a conversation with her about commitment. He told the girl that she would be his highest earthly responsibility, and wanted the same in return. (Again, I emphasize that this isn't immediately after you meet the person.) This makes every decision about the relationship   the second highest priority next to God.

Matt and his current girlfriend were going through a challenge where she had been offered a major promotion at work, which was good, but if she accepted the new job she would be putting in much longer work weeks. The new working hours would put a strain on their time together, most likely hurting the relationship. Therefore, they had a candid but difficult conversation about her work promotion. I know they argued back and forth about their priorities for a couple of weeks. But whereas most relationships would have ended at this point, they were able to focus on their priorities and be closer at the end of the process.

Matt's girlfriend did end up taking the job. Then after two months of working long hours, she put in her notice and quit. She realized working the long hours was making all of her other priorities (including God) take a back seat. She eventually got a new job with less pay, but also less stress on their relationship.

If Matt hadn't had his conversation with her about putting their relationship as the second highest priority (next to God), she might have taken the glamorous job, worked it thinking she needed to do so to get ahead, and eventually they would have broken up. A few years down the road, she would be wealthier for sure, but her life wouldn't be where she wants it to be.

She would be burned out at a job that she doesn't want to do forever, probably be single, and have an excuse like, "The timing wasn't right" for why she and this great guy, Matt, didn't make it a few years ago.

I never had a conversation with Rachel about commitment to the relationship being the highest priority behind God. Basically, she would have a responsibility, idea, or job that would put a strain on our relationship, and I would not know how to confront her about it. I wanted to support her dreams, but I feared she would leave, so I generally didn't rock the boat. When Rachel was applying to graduate schools, I assumed she was going locally in Atlanta. There are plenty of schools here that would fit her needs. So one evening I asked her, "Where are you applying?" She responded, "Vanderbilt, Texas, Emory, I haven't finished the Yale application yet!" I'm sure she wanted me to be supportive, but I wasn't. All I could think was, "Is this girl going to get close to me and then leave in six months?" I didn't want to rock the boat so I just let it go. It wasn't long after that she was also looking at teaching positions at new schools. It was clear from the variety of places where she was applying that I wasn't as high a priority as her teaching was.

I'm sure I probably made her feel uncomfortable as well, with music and other career choices. I wasn't always putting her in the second priority spot, so feelings were hurt both ways.

It would have been uncomfortable, but I should have done what Matt did once we decided to be serious. We should have talked about what both of our top priorities were, and then made sure we were both committed at the same level.

I admire Rachel for her big dreams and goals. That's one reason I was attracted to her, and probably a big reason she was attracted to me as well. But we could have said, "Hey, let's chase our dreams together and try to stay within an hour of where we currently live." We could both have done that effectively. And if that ever changed, if I needed to move to Nashville for music, or she needed to move for her career, we could have had that conversation down the road. As it was, sometimes I was an unsupportive and frustrated boyfriend. She was a girlfriend who couldn't commit, and sometimes didn't have a clue as to the trade-offs she wanted to make in life.

If we would have had the priorities-and-commitment conversation, we might have realized we weren't as serious as we thought, and not made a strong commitment to each other. Then I would have avoided getting overly attached to her. Such a conversation on priorities and commitment will have serious consequences on the outcome of the relationship.

In the end, I wasn't a top priority for Rachel behind God. She hadn't thought through which priorities were going to be most important to her, and quickly friends, career, and other dreams were in her ear telling her to put me as a lower priority. And she did. If I had been her second priority the week we broke up, she would have called, texted, and communicated with me instead of just ignoring me when she was "busy" with other friends on vacation.

I can hear the protests now from people saying, "Your family should be higher," or "My BFF should be higher!" Never dump family or friends, but know which way you will choose when they come into conflict. If you put family above partner that is fine, but when conflict arises (and it always does between the two), don't be surprised when your relationship doesn't work out. If you are reading this and are under 18 years old, or don't support yourself financially, listen to your parents. They should be ahead of any guy or girl.

I divide relationships into four levels:

1. **Newly Dating** - There is very little commitment at this point. You are just getting to know each other. (All high school relationships are here.)

2. **Seriously Dating** - This is when you need to have the commitment conversation.

3. **Engaged** - God first. Relationship second.

4. **Married** - God first. Relationship second.

Basically, what will be your second highest priority behind God? Your work? Your family? Your workout routine? Your parents? Your best friend? Or will it be your relationship?

Two examples may help. I remember one Friday Rachel had a friend coming in from California and they were going to spend the evening having dinner and going ice skating. Rachel called me on her way home from work, "Hey, are you busy? I can swing by before I meet my friend." I felt very valued that she would want to spend 45 minutes of free time in her day with me. She rarely got to see this friend and I was happy see her go off and have a good time. In that situation we did a good job of making our relationship a priority; I got to see her, and she also saw her friend.

Not long after that, however, we both had a free evening and we had talked earlier in the day about having dinner. In the afternoon, she sent me a text that she was going to work out with a friend and might be slightly late. No worries, I'm a flexible guy. I got off work and home by about 6:30, and texted to see where she was. I found out she was 45 minutes away in the middle of a workout. She had a gym she belonged to five minutes away. So I didn't even get to pick her up until close to 9:00. I had been waiting two and a half hours.

As I picked her up I asked, "Why did you work out 45 minutes away?" She responded, "I didn't realize it was that far, and that is where my friend lives." I didn't tell her this (I probably should have), but she put her friend, who she sees often, ahead of me. We had a very late dinner and I had planned to take her to a spot to watch the sunset. By the time we got there it was dark, and she fell asleep as we sat there. It was a crummy evening. She apologized and we moved on.

Those are two simple everyday examples of how relationship priorities can make your life easy and enjoyable, or stressful and frustrating. Even with this guideline, however, conflicts will happen. Relationships are sometimes messy. You can't always be perfect, but knowing where your commitment level stands helps you know what to shoot for. Unless you have the relationship first, behind God, I do not believe it will last. Also, I think the priority problem is a big contributor to many divorces and dull lifeless marriages down the line as well.

Jesus said it well when he was teaching about priorities: "So do not worry, saying, 'What shall we eat?' or 'What shall we drink?' or 'What shall we wear?' For the pagans run after all these things, and your heavenly Father knows that you need them. But seek first his kingdom and his righteousness, and all these things will be given to you as well" (Matthew 6: 31-33). Jesus was saying put Me first, and all the rest will fall into place. My addition to that: Put Jesus first, and your relationship with your significant other second, and the rest will fall into place.

After Matt and I finished eating, I made Matt laugh by telling him that a few months ago when we both were in new relationships, "I thought Rachel and I had many fewer problems and would last, whereas you [Matt] and your new girlfriend had tons of problems and wouldn't make it." The difference between the relationships was that Matt and his girlfriend were committed to putting God first and the relationship second, while Rachel and I weren't. Now Matt is in a solid relationship that has lasted and will last as long as they keep God first and relationship second.

Point to Remember:

When you are entering a serious relationship, have a conversation with your partner about priorities: God first, relationship second.

Level	Commitment Level	Description
1	Newly Dating	Getting to know each other.
2	Seriously Dating	Time to have the commitment conversation.
3	Engaged	God first. Relationship second.
4	Married	God first. Relationship second.

Chapter 35

Sex

This is the chapter everyone has been waiting for. Most of the single people reading this want me to say, "Do whatever you want! Physical is just physical. It doesn't matter." Most pastors want me to yell from the rooftop, "DON'T HAVE SEX!" The dads with daughters want me to say, "Everyone should be wearing turtlenecks and long pants regardless of the weather, and no touching any boys, ever!"

Single people hear all kinds of differing views on how they should be treating their bodies physically. As we learned in the "Stats" section of the introduction, 80% of evangelical Christian singles 18-30 have already had sex. (And the number goes higher as the age goes up, as would be expected.)

Most people who enter the dating world are either totally naive about sex, or have experience and regrets. I was super naive. I assumed (incorrectly) that most single people in the pews didn't run around sleeping with a bunch of people.

So once I started dating, I did what many Christ-followers do: I tried to do as much as I could without breaking the rules. Which leads to breaking the rules. So I basically tried to stay away from any activities that could possibly impregnate somebody, and did pretty much anything else I wanted. I thought, "Hey, I am following what the pastors are usually saying, 'Don't have sex,' so I'm good, and I'm not going to impregnate someone. So I have nothing to worry about."

That was until I met Maggie. We met at church. She had been taking her faith seriously for a couple of years, and I didn't suspect there was anything to worry about. She prayed, read her Bible, and served at church faithfully. Physically, I stuck to the pastor's message above. "Don't do any impregnating activities and everything will be fine."

All was going well until she told me one evening on a date, "I have something I need to tell you. I have an STD." She went on to explain one of her previous boyfriends had cheated on her, acquired the disease, and then gave it to her. Also, it was permanent. There was medication to help with the breakouts, but she would have this condition for the rest of her life.

I was absolutely speechless. In my naive Christian bubble, I assumed that people who had STDs were the people who were with someone different every weekend, not some girl who let her guard down and trusted the wrong guy! (This is probably obvious to many readers, but there are people like me who grow up and live in a bubble.)

Maggie was a crying mess at that moment. She said, "I understand if you don't want us to date anymore." Me? I was just stumbling around trying to take all this in. After talking about it for awhile, I realized, "What if I have acquired this disease?" I started asking her questions about her condition. She kept reassuring me, "You're fine. You don't have it." I agreed it would be a one in an million chance if I did get it from what we had done, but there was still an ever so slight chance. I just kept thinking, "How could this girl get that physical with me and not disclose what she had? She may have put me in harm's way." I couldn't say that to her that evening because she was already a mess, but I was really hurt and irritated.

So I went home and looked up information about STDs on the internet. I learned that there are 20 million new STD infections in the United States every year. And out of a population of about 320 million people in the U.S., 110 million of them have an STD.[1] That means about one out of three Americans currently has a sexually transmitted disease. I found that shocking!

---

1   http://www.livescience.com/48100-sexually-transmitted-infections-50-states-map.html

Next, I wanted to be sure I wasn't one of the one in three. So I looked online and found there are three common ways to get checked for STDs:

1. Primary Care Doctors - They will give you the test, and bill you for a normal doctor's visit with a lab test.

2. County Health Clinics - They have discounted rates, and a quick google search will show your nearest location.

3. Online STD Testing - Usually costs about $200. You sign up online and receive an email from a doctor (or healthcare professionals). They send you to a lab-testing facility near you. If the test results are normal, they notify you via email. If the results show that you have an STD, then a doctor will call you to explain your options.

I decided to get the Online STD Testing. It was very discreet. I thought, "No one would ever know." I paid my $200 and went to a lab facility down the street and was checked out in five minutes. Two weeks later I received an email saying, "Everything is good." What a relief! I was okay.

Back to Maggie. I called up a close friend, who is a doctor, and asked him about Maggie's STD. He seemed very casual, "Adam, I see this all the time.

It's really not a big deal. Yes, her STD is permanent, but I wouldn't let it bother your overall decision about this girl." I had a decision to make: "Would I let Maggie's past get in the way of our future?" I decided that if she was the girl for me, I was going to take the consequences.

Other people in my situation might have different reactions. We all have to make that decision on our own. There isn't a right or wrong answer. I can understand why someone wouldn't want to deal with an STD forever.

I hope that my being okay with the situation brings hope to the people who are reading this and do have an STD. Even I, in my little Christian bubble, would be willing to overlook and take the consequences of someone's past indiscretion if she was who I wanted for a wife.

Maggie, however, should have disclosed her condition earlier, before we had any physical contact. If you have an STD, you need to share that information with whomever you are dating BEFORE you get physical with them.

Maggie and I didn't make it much longer as a couple after that. Other challenges arose and we decided to move on.

After the relationship was over, I realized I needed a new game plan for how I behaved with girls physically. I knew I didn't want to put myself in that situation again until I had a ring on my finger and had permanently said, "I do!" As we discussed earlier in the book, there aren't many guidelines in the Bible for dating, and especially for how to handle the physical part of dating.

Most logical people will agree that being physical with someone changes the relationship. George Costanza once said in *Seinfeld*, "Borrowing money from a friend is like having sex. It just completely changes the relationship." Even if you kiss someone, the relationship changes, and becomes more serious. The level of emotional attachment grows rapidly when you are with someone intimately.

So I decided to look at things pragmatically. I thought when people are engaged and about to be married, being somewhat physically involved is understandable. You are already emotionally attached to that person. You are already very committed to that person. And your partner should be committed and emotionally attached to you as well.

But when someone gets physical early in the relationship, you don't know if your partner is committed to you. Getting too physical too early sets you up for being hurt. The physical closeness causes emotional closeness; without the commitment you are set up for heartache.

So my new suggested game plan for being physical while dating is this:

1. **Newly Dating** - Keep all of your clothes on. (Reminder: High school students should be in stage one.)
2. **Seriously Dating** - Moderate level of physical intimacy is okay.
3. **Engaged** - Stay away from the baby-making activity, but higher physical level is okay.
4. **Married** - Make babies.

Basically, keep your level of physical intimacy on the same level as your commitment level.[2]

In my experience, it's easier to follow through when I have a goal or standard. Know how far you are going to go physically before you get in that situation

---

2   I have been told hundreds of times, "The Bible says sex outside of marriage is sin." So while writing this chapter about sex, I studied the relevant New Testament verses in the original Greek. The word most often translated fornication in the NIV Bible is the word *pornia* in Greek. *Pornia* means "unlawful sexual activity." In the Old Testament law, Leviticus 18 lists unacceptable sexual practices. But sex before marriage isn't on the list. I assume that sex before marriage wasn't as widespread as it is today. Some scholars argue that sex before marriage is implied in various New Testament verses. That may be true, but different people interpret the verses different ways.

and it will be easier to stay where you need to be. If you're trying to decide how far to go in the moment, you will probably make a bad decision.

If you think I am off base, and that a dating couple should not go so far physically, by all means do less. You are sensible and safe. I'm not trying to convince people they should do anything they don't believe is right, or aren't comfortable with. I am trying to convince people who don't have a plan, and haven't been treating their bodies and emotions well, to think about consequences and set a goal. 1 Corinthians 6:19-20 says, "Do you not know that your bodies are temples of the Holy Spirit, who is in you, whom you have received from God? You are not your own; you were bought at a price. Therefore honor God with your bodies." You are valuable! Treat your body well!

One comment I often hear is, "I just can't control myself. How do you not just lose control in intimate situations?" First off, I haven't been perfect. I'm not trying to wag my finger at you because you "should" do something. I'm only trying to get you to have a plan and follow through with it because if you do, you will make better dating decisions and have less heartache.

If you are struggling in this area, avoid temptation. Protect yourself. If I am roaming around town late at night, I know I need to be home by midnight. I have made some bad decisions after midnight. (If I am at a friend's house, or in a safer environment, I don't worry as much about my midnight curfew.)

Also, you have God on your side to help you out. 1 Corinthians 10:13 says, "No temptation has overtaken you except what is common to mankind. And God is faithful; he will not let you be tempted beyond what you can bear. But when you are tempted, he will also provide a way out so that you can endure it."

An example of this in my life occurred when I played in an outdoor hockey tournament in Northern Wisconsin a few years ago. (Yes, I played hockey outside in weather as cold as -24 degrees Fahrenheit.) My team had gone to another local team's hockey game one evening, and on our way home we stopped at a restaurant. At the restaurant I struck up a conversation with a local girl. She was a school teacher and very attractive. We got out on the dance floor and were having a good time. My carload of friends were ready to leave, but I was still having fun. So they walked by and told me to give them a call when I was finished and they would pick me up. (It was after midnight, which should have put me on guard.)

This girl and I hung out and danced for another hour or so when she asked, "Hey, why don't you just come home with me tonight?" I didn't know her. I didn't know anything about her. My first good decision that evening was dodging that question and telling her I needed to go back to the place I was staying.

When I called my friend's number to ask him to pick me up, no one answered. I called a different friend's phone, no answer. I tried multiple times and could not get an answer. It was really late at this point, and I asked the bartender, "Hey, can you get me a cab?" He responded, "We don't have any cabs in this town," and walked off. I thought to myself, "How do people get home around here?" I couldn't find anyone to give me a ride. It was so cold outside that I wouldn't have lasted long if I had tried to walk back, and I had no one to get me where I needed to go.

So I walked over to the lodge across the street to see if anyone there could give me a ride. It was totally quiet. Not a noise or a person anywhere. There was a chair in the foyer of the lodge, and as I sat in it for a few minutes, I realized, "This might be where I spend the rest of the night." Not a good feeling. So I walked back across the street to the restaurant where I had spent most of the evening.

As I was walking across the road, a school bus pulled into the parking lot. I ran after it and flagged it down, asking the driver, "Hey, I just need a ride a couple of miles down the street. Can you give me a ride?" He said, "Yeah, sure." I hopped on the bus, and five minutes later I was walking through the door of the place where my team was staying. God fulfilled His promise. When I was tempted, He provided a way out. He provided a school bus in the middle of nowhere Wisconsin at three in the morning to get me home.

I made plenty of bad decisions that night, but no matter how deep I was into the evening, or how bad the decisions I had made up to that point, God still provided a way out. Whatever situation you are in, whatever you are being tempted with, God will provide a way out. He did that for me in Wisconsin, and will do it for you as well.

Points to Remember:

1. Keep your level of physical intimacy on the same level as your commitment level.

2. Don't put yourself in bad situations. When you are tempted, know that God will always provide you with a way out.

3. About 1 in 3 people in the United States currently have an STD. Many don't even know they are infected. If you have been sexually active, get tested. If you disregard the advice in this book, and are sexually active, get tested regularly.

Level	Commitment Level	Physical Level
1	Newly Dating	Keep all of your clothes on.
2	Seriously Dating	Moderate level of physical intimacy is okay.
3	Engaged	No baby-making activity, but higher physical level okay.
4	Married	Make babies.

Chapter 36

Emotions

I went to a Halloween party at my friend Macy's house, and I thought a costume was optional. I didn't dress up and it turned out I was the only person there not in a costume. I eventually stopped by to talk with Macy, who was dressed as a mermaid, to tell her thanks for inviting me. I'd known her for about a year, and we hung out together occasionally. I casually asked about her week, when the tone shifted and she said, "I'm going to die alone." Macy is a very tough woman, not the kind to be overly dramatic. I had never heard her talk like this before. "No you're not," I said. "Lots of guys want to be in a relationship with you." She responded, "I know, but I don't believe I am ever going to be able to let any of them in." Basically she was saying, "I don't think I could ever trust a guy with my heart again." (She had been married before and it didn't work out.) I just kept reassuring her the best I could that night.

That conversation with Macy stayed on my mind for the next few days. I understood that she was hurt and wounded, but she clearly did not want to be alone. Deep down, she wanted to be in a relationship. Then I realized that she was trying to trust someone with her whole heart right away. Here is the principle I thought of after we talked: If she has only gone out with a guy a couple of times, she should only trust him emotionally a little bit. Then as the relationship grows, let the emotion grow with it.

The movie *Pitch Perfect* does a good job illustrating this point. Beca is hurt by her parents' divorce, and doesn't let anyone near her because she might get hurt again. By the end of the movie she starts letting people into her life again.

Trusting someone emotionally is a choice, not a feeling. And it is very tough to keep your emotions on the same level as your commitment. There are two ways to get in trouble with your heart emotionally.

1. **Moving too quickly.** I made the mistake of letting my heart get too attached too quickly with Natalie (from chapter 2). We were not dating very long and I was letting my heart get way too attached. I needed to focus on just getting to know her, and after I knew her better, I could accurately either let my heart fall or move on to someone else.

2. **Moving too slowly or not letting your emotions move at all.** This describes Macy. She was letting the hurt from the past paralyze her emotions. It is risky to trust someone, but life gets very lonely if you are all by yourself. Moving too slowly can be worse than moving too quickly.

I believe this lack of trust happened to Rachel and me at the end of our relationship as well. She had been hurt emotionally in the past, and when she felt that I was unsupportive, she chose to end the relationship. But she also missed out.

For example, a few months after Rachel and I broke up, I visited a friend in Singapore. Rachel loved to travel and had visited there before. If we were still together, she might have gone with me on this trip. She was fascinated that you could be in Singapore and drive across a bridge and be in Malaysia, a different country, all in the same hour. (I always told her you can drive across from the U.S. to Mexico or Canada, but that never seemed to resonate.)

During my time in Singapore, my buddy (and his lady friend) suggested we cross the border from Singapore to Malaysia for the weekend. It happened to be a national holiday, and the border crossing was packed. People were everywhere, and nobody knew what to do. We passed through customs, but the buses that bring people across the bridge to Malaysia were overwhelmed. So the Singapore officials told people, "Start walking!" We walked across the bridge to the Malaysian side of the border crossing! Rachel would have loved that. My friends and I walked across the bridge to the other country, just as she had envisioned so many times.

After a two hour cab ride across Malaysia, followed by a ferry ride, we arrived on Tioman Island. We were staying at a resort, but unlike big hotels in America, this resort consisted of 15 bungalows. So we had an entire pristine private beach and were only sharing it with a handful of other people.

I was sitting on an oceanside chair when a staff member from the resort introduced herself as the dive instructor and asked, "Hey, would you like to scuba dive? I have time to take you tomorrow." I responded, "I've never done that before. I'm not certified." She went on to explain that the rules are loose in Malaysia, and if I signed a release form, that was all she needed. (I can only imagine the lawsuits that would happen from this arrangement in the U.S.)

The next day I had a unique experience. People come every year from all over the world to dive near Tioman Island. The dive instructor showed my friends and me how to operate the gear, move in the water, and how to equalize the air pressure in our ears. Then we headed out. I saw hundreds of fish that were every color of the rainbow. I saw clownfish and anemones, just like in the movie *Finding Nemo*. Also, I saw many different types of coral and even a stingray. It was an incredible experience I will remember for the rest of my life.

On the plane ride home, 18 hours in total flight time, I couldn't stop thinking about Rachel, and how much she would have loved that trip. She missed out because she decided not to let someone get close. She missed walking over that bridge because she didn't want to let me into her life. She never saw Nemo because she let the pain of her past control her decisions. When you choose not to let people who are good into your life, you miss out on great experiences and opportunities.

The pain is easy to feel when somebody you love disappoints you, but look at the past and how that person has treated you. No one is perfect. Sometimes you have to trust that the people you love still have your best interests in mind. If you choose not to trust, you might not get hurt by them, but you will also be alone.

Your emotional level, just like your physical level, needs to stay in line with your commitment. If you've barely dated someone, keep your heart in check. But if someone has been good to you for awhile, increase your trust.

Point to Remember:

Some people will need to slow their emotions down, others will need to open their hearts up, but keep your commitment level and your emotional level at the same place.

Level	Commitment Level	Emotional Level
1	Newly Dating	Keep your heart in check. DO NOT let your heart go.
2	Seriously Dating	Time to start letting your heart go, bit by bit.
3	Engaged	Your heart should be "all in" for your future spouse.
4	Married	Love your spouse, even if you aren't feeling it.

Chapter 37

Spiritual

The traditional message from the church about the spiritual side of dating is, "Do not be yoked together with unbelievers. For what do righteousness and wickedness have in common? Or what fellowship can light have with darkness?" (2 Corinthians 6:14). That is good advice. A less churchy way of saying the same thing would be, "Date people who have similar values to you. If you don't have similar values, you are going to be fighting each other all the time."

That is easy to say from the pulpit at church. But putting it into practice can be a challenge. How do you really know what someone's relationship with Christ is like, and deep down what that person's values are? It's not like sports, where there are scoreboards, or school, where there are grades. (Can you imagine, "I won't date anyone who believes in Jesus with a grade lower than a "B"?) I've met girls who grew up in church, went to Christian schools, and knew exactly what they were supposed to say and when to say it. But once I got to know them, there was very little faith there. How do I discern who is serious about her faith and who is not?

Then I heard a sermon from Andy Stanley where he mentioned the best thing you could do for your marriage is pray together out loud. He cited a study that discovered that fewer than 8% of Christian couples pray together.[1] I started asking couples I knew if they prayed together, and was surprised at how few do. I find it interesting that people get completely naked together and think nothing of it, but won't pray together because it is "awkward."

The good thing about praying together is we shouldn't just do it because Andy Stanley says so. A 1993 Gallup Poll showed: "The divorce rate among couples who go to church together regularly is 1 out of 2—the same as among unbelievers. But the divorce rate among couples who pray together daily is 1 out of 1,153."[2] Are you kidding me?!? A less than 1% divorce rate among couples who pray together! Praying together out loud will give you a 99% chance of making it. A 99% chance of preventing divorce! If you take nothing else away from this book, pray with your spouse out loud daily when married.

---

1   http://www.familylife.com/articles/topics/marriage/staying-married/growing-spiritually/one-simple-habit-that-will-transform-your-marriage

2   Cheryl Sacks, *The Prayer Saturated Church* (Colorado Springs: NavPress, 2007), kindle edition.

When you pray with someone, it creates intimacy. You better understand what is important to that person, and what is bothering that person. When you pray with them and for them you show that you care for them. And it gets God, who is all powerful, involved in your lives.

Now how does this information translate to dating?

If you are just getting to know each other, only pray before meals. You don't want to get too intimate too quickly. This is the time in the relationship when I listen for clues as to how seriously a girl takes her relationship with Christ. If I hear, "While doing devotions today..." or "We've been going over...in my small group," those are great signs. They tell me the girl is probably taking her relationship with Christ seriously.

If I have gone out with someone several times and haven't heard her talk about Christ, Bible, devotions, small group, sermons, or anything scriptural applying to her life, then I put a pause on whether we should be continuing our relationship. I'm not saying the girl isn't saved or a good person, but I want someone who is growing in her faith and relationship with Christ.

If you are a Christian and dating seriously, pray together occasionally with your partner. If you are both willing to pray together out loud, you show that you take your relationship with God and with each other seriously. Also, I think reading the Bible together is a good idea. A place I have started in the past with a date is Proverbs. The ideas there are easy to grasp, not too controversial, and you can read a chapter a day.

I have never been engaged, but when I am, I hope to be praying with that person out loud on a regular basis. That is really the prep time for how your marriage will function. I will also be sure to be going through premarital counseling. People who counsel young couples regularly can help set you up for success.

I believe if I keep my spiritual level in line with my commitment level, when I am married I will be praying regularly with my wife. We will want our marriage to be in the 99% success-rate category.

For those who need some help in what to say during your prayers, Andy Stanley described these three tips for how to pray with your spouse:

1. Short and awkward is better than long and flawless.
2. Pray with each other, not at each other.
3. Pray together with your children. Pray together for your children.

If this is your first time praying with someone out loud, it might be awkward at first. Just grab the hand of your partner and say, "Lord, we're praying. Help us today. Amen." That is a great start! You don't have to be perfect.

Points to Remember:

1. Keep your relationship's spiritual level in line with your commitment level.

2. The couples that pray together stay together. Fewer than 1% of couples who pray regularly together get divorced.

Level	Commitment Level	Spiritual Level
1	Newly Dating	Pray before meals.
2	Seriously Dating	Begin praying out loud together.
3	Engaged	Regularly pray out loud and read the Bible together.
4	Married	Daily pray and read the Bible together.

Chapter 38

Friends

Here is a typical conversation you might hear at a restaurant among single friends:

Adam: Hey, how's it going? Good to see you guys.

Everyone else: Hey, good to see you.

Adam: Is Sean coming?

Mario: I don't think he's going to be here. It's been awhile since I've seen him. I don't think I've seen him in a couple of months.

Jerry: Yeah, I haven't seen him since he started dating the photography girl. What's her name again?

Adam: Emily. You can tell she's a photographer. Her Facebook pictures with him are impressive.

Jerry: Yeah, he doesn't look like the beast he usually is.

[Everyone Laughs]

Mario: I guess we'll see Sean again when he breaks up with her, or when we get invited to the wedding.

I have often had that kind of conversation with friends. When single friends start dating someone, they often mysteriously disappear from the face of the Earth. Their new significant other crowds everyone else out.

Going from being single, and seeing many friends, to being in a relationship can be a tough and messy transition. Some friends have been hanging out regularly for years, but eventually when you are getting serious with someone, you have to put them on the back burner. And that can be very tough to manage.

Sometimes friends aren't fond of the person you are dating, and your new date isn't fond of your friends. That is natural because they are both competing for your time and attention. A group of single people will often want to do different activities from what a couple wants to do. So naturally you start to drift apart.

I have been with a group of guys spending Friday nights seeing how many ice cream sandwiches we can eat in 3 minutes, but most girls don't find that attractive or want to be around it. On the flip side, I have sat at lunch tables where girls are talking a million miles an hour, all at the same time, about the TV show *The Bachelor*. By the end of the lunch, I am running for the exit.

How do you balance friends and a relationship?

If you are just beginning to date someone, you shouldn't be ditching your friends. If you go on a date on Friday, see your friends on Saturday. If the new relationship doesn't work out, you will need your friends. Don't ditch them.

If you are seriously dating someone, however, then start separating from your friend group, and make your partner a higher priority.

If you are engaged, life moves fast. A lot of people work, see their significant other, plan the wedding, and that is about it. Friends are put on the back burner, which makes sense. It's a natural progression that the partner is taking over for what the friends used to do—talking, supporting, and helping you with life.

If you are married, get ready to not see single friends as much. I often see people who have massive numbers of bridesmaids and groomsmen, then a few years later they barely talk to any of them. It's sad in a way, but if you are about 30 you have seen this happen many times. You've either been in the wedding, or have known the couple well, then they just disappear. You watch their life on Facebook and Instagram, but you aren't in it. Married couples often find other married couples to hang out with.

Point to Remember:

While in a dating relationship, keep your friends level in line with your commitment level. See the chart below:

Level	Commitment Level	Friends Level
1	Newly Dating	Regularly see your friends. Don't forget them.
2	Seriously Dating	Start making your partner a higher priority than friends.
3	Engaged	Life moves fast. Often not much time for friends.
4	Married	You will probably hang out with other married couples.

Chapter 39

Time

Being single affords you incredible freedom with your time. If I feel like driving 45 minutes to a steakhouse north of town to eat dinner, I just do it. If I feel like going to the river to run, I can do that, too. If I feel like going to the Notre Dame football game watch party at The Wing Factory, I can do that. If I want to do…basically anything, I have the freedom with my time to do that.

When I invite my married male friends to an event, they either don't come, leave early, or say, "Let me call my wife and see if I can come." Then he will be made fun of by all the single guys there, and probably leave soon after. I may laugh at that, but I agree: the amount of time spent together as a married couple is very important.

Time management is an important issue when you are dating, too. You're not single and free, but you're not married and locked down either.

Time and proximity lead to deeper relationships. The more quality time you spend with someone, the deeper your relationship will be. So the higher your commitment level is, the more time you should be spending together as a couple.

Point to Remember:

Keep the amount of time you spend with your partner in line with your commitment level. Just as in previous chapters:

Level	Commitment Level	Friends Level
1	Newly Dating	Don't spend 24/7 with your new significant other.
2	Seriously Dating	Shorten or quit activities that strain your relationship.
3	Engaged	Work, plan your wedding, be with your partner.
4	Married	Your time is not your own.

Chapter 40

Levels

The best way to date is to know your commitment level, and keep every other facet of your relationship at that level. We have already seen how this idea works with your physical intimacy level, emotional level, spiritual level, relationships with friends, and use of time. But this idea applies to many other areas of your relationship: communication, disclosure, money, life vision, living situation, shared activities, dreams, goals, and I could go on. This is the New Game Plan for Christian Dating.

Any time you have an issue with your partner, or you don't know what your goal is, go back to where your commitment level is and keep the issue at that level. Dating can be messy, and every relationship is different. That makes it difficult to have stringent rules that apply to large masses of people. Occasionally, your relationship will probably get out of line and may need some adjustment. Every time your relationship takes a step forward will be a new learning experience. But if you both move forward, with every aspect of your relationship in line with your commitment level, then you have a great game plan for successful dating. You won't just be wandering around trying to figure it out as you go along and creating regrets along the way.

The New Game Plan is not the easiest way to date, but it will move you forward and both of you can become better people along the way. You will be growing closer to God as you pray together regularly out loud. You will be trusting each other emotionally more and more. You will be physically becoming more attached. You will be slowly transitioning to your partner being your emotional support and best friend. You will be becoming a couple.

I can often tell when a friend of mine is close to being engaged because his use of pronouns will change from "I" to "We." A guy who is single or is still thinking like a single person will say things like, "I'm going to the game on Saturday, and Tracy is coming with me." or "I'm going to my parents in North Carolina for Thanksgiving." But when someone is in a relationship that is getting very serious, the pronouns change to "we". "We are going to the lake this weekend," or "We are taking a cooking class on Tuesdays." "I" and "We" are simple words, but anytime I have a friend make the switch from "I" to "We," I know engagement is soon to come.

Deep down, I think most of us want to be a "We." Life is just better when we have someone to share it with. As usual, God knows what He is doing creating relationships and marriage. All the way back to Adam and Eve, the book of Genesis says, "That is why a man leaves his father and mother and is united to his wife, and they become one flesh" (Genesis 2:24). That verse is quoted in many marriage ceremonies because two "I"s are being transformed into a "We."

Point to Remember:

With any area of your relationship, keep it on the same level as your commitment level.

Newly Dating:

Commitment Level	Getting to know each other.
Physical Level	Keep all of your clothes on.
Emotional Level	Keep your heart in check. DO NOT let your heart go.
Spiritual Level	Pray before meals.
Friends Level	Regularly see your friends. Don't forget them.
Time Level	Do not spend 24/7 with your new significant other.

Seriously Dating:

Commitment Level	Time to have the commitment conversation.
Physical Level	Moderate level of physical intimacy is okay.
Emotional Level	Time to start letting your heart go, bit by bit.
Spiritual Level	Begin praying out loud together.
Friends Level	Start making your partner a higher priority than friends.
Time Level	Shorten or quit activities that strain your relationship.

Engaged:

Commitment Level	God first. Relationship second.
Physical Level	No baby-making activity, but higher physical level okay.
Emotional Level	Your heart should be "all in" for your future spouse.
Spiritual Level	Regularly pray out loud and read the Bible together.
Friends Level	Life moves fast. Often not much time for friends.
Time Level	Work, plan your wedding, be with your partner.

Married:

Commitment Level	God first. Relationship second.
Physical Level	Make babies.
Emotional Level	Love your spouse, even if you aren't feeling it.
Spiritual Level	Daily pray and read the Bible together.
Friends Level	You will probably hang out with other married couples.
Time Level	Your time is not your own.

Section 4
Study Questions

1. Do you know the commitment level of your dating relationship? What priorities are more important to you than your dating relationship?

2. Do you have a plan for how you will handle the physical aspect of your dating relationships? Have you talked about this with your partner?

3. Remember that 1 out of 3 Americans currently has an STD. Do you need to get checked?

4. Look at the charts on pages 228-230. Which aspects of dating relationships do you have the most difficulty keeping in line with your commitment level?

5. If you are seriously dating, engaged, or married, are you praying together with your partner out loud? Are you reading the Bible together?

Chapter 41

Conclusion

Fast forward six months after my breakup with Rachel.

I was sitting in Arby's eating lunch before I headed to the one o'clock service at church. I could see my reflection in the window next to me, which led me to think about how I had been single and content for the past six months.

Twenty minutes later, I arrived at church and sat in my usual section. I looked over and about 30 feet from me, one section over, Rachel walked in with a couple of her friends. I was not ready for that.

I had a lot on my plate at that moment. I was recording the song, *Don't Be Strong Tonight*, which was about us breaking up, I had been asked to help write songs for an up-and-coming singer whose father was a famous Nashville star, and the corporation where I worked two days a week had just been bought by a private equity firm. I did not need more stress.

I thought to myself, "She never comes to this service!" I sat there for a minute stunned and ill at ease. I thought, "I don't want to sit here and be looking over and thinking about her rejecting me all service. I'll move to the other side of the auditorium. Problem solved." I got up and walked out of the auditorium into the hallway to find a different section. When I looked up, Rachel had just walked into the hallway from her section and was standing right in front of me!

"Hey, Adam, how are you doing? How are your parents?" she asked. For someone who didn't want to meet my parents six months ago, she suddenly seemed interested in them. I told her a little about what they were doing. Then I asked what she had been up to. She told me about her new job, which was much better than her last teaching job. I noticed she looked confident and in control. She looked older, but a good older. And she had the same beautiful green eyes that cut right through me.

She asked how I was doing. Which is good because I had some impressive stuff to tell her. "I am recording another song this weekend. With the same production team as last time." Now I tried to look super relaxed and casual when I told her about the songwriting for the up-and-coming Nashville artist. (She had heard of the artist.) "Wow, that's big!" she responded.

We continued to talk through the first songs of the service that had already started in the auditorium next to us. We ended by her saying, "It was great catching up with you!" I said, "Yeah, it was good." And she walked back into the auditorium. I walked down the hall to the bathroom and tried to pull myself together. I was shaking. I thought I had my emotions in control with this girl, but clearly I did not.

I walked into the other side of the auditorium and found a seat. I was still shaking. The sermon was going on now, but it sounded like adults in the Charlie Brown cartoons, just indiscernible noise. There was no way I could pay attention today. I slipped out the door early and went home.

To be honest, when I started writing the book, I was beginning my relationship with Rachel, and I thought by this point in the book she would have my ring on her left hand. That would have made the entire story come full circle and be the "live happily ever after" ending that we all love. That didn't happen, but that's okay.

I fully believe that God has a plan for me (and for you) that is good. Any time I need to be reminded of that, I look back at my long list from "God's Faithfulness to Adam" (Chapter 26). God has been faithful to me all along. I trust that He will provide the perfect spouse for me. There are dozens of stories in the Bible of God's faithfulness, and I know that if you put your trust in Him, He will be faithful to you. God always has a plan, a good plan, for your life.

King David 3000 years ago said in Psalm 23:6 (NIV), "Surely your goodness and love will follow me all the days of my life, and I will dwell in the house of the Lord forever." Every day of my life goodness and love are following me. I love that imagery. Every day, regardless of my past actions, God's grace, goodness, and love are following me. With my life, with my job, with my dating, God's goodness is creating a good path for me to follow.

Some day I will have an end to my dating story, and it will be a good one. I want to tell people, "From this point forward, I fixed as many problems and cleaned out as much baggage as possible. I became the right person for my future spouse. I was in the right environment to meet new people. I purposefully had people in my life who gave me wise dating advice. I removed wrong friends from my life, and made more time for the right friends. I leaned on God, even when circumstances looked bad. I forgave girls who offended me along the way. I always knew where the commitment level was in my relationships. I kept the physical intimacy level, emotional level, spiritual level, and every aspect of my relationships in line with where my commitment level was. And I regularly prayed out loud with my future wife." I know if I can tell this story for the rest of my dating life, I will be set up for the best marriage possible.

Five years from now, ten years from now, twenty years from now, you will be looking back and telling the story of your single and dating life. What do you want your story to be? What do you need to change now in order to have your story end the way you want?

In the space below, write down an answer to this question: **What story will you tell about your single and dating life?**

Epilogue

It's 11:32 p.m., and I am putting the final edits into this book. I can't help but think back to the introduction, and how crushed I was after my breakup with Natalie. But in that time of despair, God called me to write this book, and help others avoid the heartache I had experienced. I don't believe this book would have happened without her.

I remember my first dates with Kelly. I will forever remember our summers together and replay the good memories in my mind.

As for Jennifer, without her rejecting me, I don't believe I would have had the push to chase my dreams. I would probably be living a safe life, going into a boring but highly paid corporate job every day. Instead, I chased my dreams, and risked failure, to own my own business and become a singer-songwriter.

Rachel has been one of the biggest influences on the direction of my life. When I met her, I had a floundering real estate business, a music career that was going nowhere, and had lived like a nomad for the previous three years. She looked past all of that and poured confidence into me when the only other people who believed in me were my Mom and Dad. I felt her confidence in me so deeply that it translated into my songwriting. My songs were now deeper, stronger, and more passionate. Others took notice, and today, I am paid to write songs that get played on the radio. And finally, she inspired me to push through and get my real estate business stable and profitable. I was then able to quit my part-time corporate job and buy a new condo—this time for me to live in. Because of her influence, my life has been transformed in many ways since our first date at Flip Burger.

Even though none of these positive dating relationships ended in marriage, they propelled my life further than I could have ever gone on my own. I am now an author, and travel around speaking to churches, singles groups, youth groups, small groups, and schools about dating. (I'd like to speak to your group. Contact me: booking@adamfolsom.com.)

I hope you, too, will be able to look back on the happiest times of your life and see good memories with people you've dated, just as I do with Kelly and Rachel. I hope you will see how your life improved because they were a part of it. I hope you will be fulfilled because you've had someone to share your life with. I hope bad relationships don't leave you bitter. When you are down, I hope you don't quit. I hope you take your relationship with Christ seriously. I hope you can avoid my mistakes and learn from the stories in this book. Ultimately, I hope you date.

Takeaways for Parents

What do you want your child's dating story to be? Your children, whether teenagers, young adults, or just plain adults, are dating in a very different world from yours. New technology is probably moving faster than you are, and your child will have to deal with pressures in dating that you can't imagine. The best way to set your kids up for success is to be proactive.

Encourage your child to be the right person. Are the tv, movies, and entertainment you allow in your house showing your children how to be the right person for the spouse of their dreams? Is the music your kids listen to respecting women? What kind of respect is your child giving you? That is the respect he will be giving his future spouse as well.

Encourage your kids to surround themselves with people who will help them make good decisions. My Mom and Dad often said, "As parents, we knew we were going to need help." They weren't saying they were doing a bad job as parents, but rather they knew I would need other mentors along the way.

In my case, I needed people like my friend Dan from college, to help me make good decisions during my college years. Are you encouraging your children to hang out with positive people, or are you just sending them to Sunday School once a week and hoping everything turns out okay?

Dad knew I would need people like Darrell to point me in the right direction with real estate. He knew I would need people like Peter and Dionne to get me in shape musically. Are you encouraging your kids to be involved in positive activities, or just expecting the after school program to deal with them until you get home? Both of my parents knew I would need kids' pastors, youth pastors, college pastors, and adult pastors to direct me spiritually. Are you in a church with a vibrant children's program, middle school group, and youth group? Or are you just dragging them to a service they think is boring once a week? Your children need other kids at church their age to grow and go through life with. Make this a very high priority when choosing a church to attend.

If you want your kids to have a strong marriage, show them by example. The stronger your marriage is, the easier it will be for your kids. "Studies indicate that daughters of divorced parents have a 60-percent higher divorce rate in marriages than children of non-divorced parents, and sons have a 35-percent higher divorce rate."[1] The fewer family problems you give your kids to carry around in life, the better their dating

---

1   https://mom.me/kids/6576-effect-divorced-parents-childs-future-relationships/

and marriage will be. It's easier for me to know what a positive committed relationship looks like, because I've seen one modeled. If you are struggling with your marriage, get some help. There are hundreds of marriage books available.

I have seen many people (including my parents who have been married 38 years) get counseling when needed. Asking for help working out problems doesn't make you weak, it makes you strong.

And finally, pray together out loud with your spouse, and pray together out loud for your children. When children see their parents pray, it shows them that marriage and Christ are a priority. When you pray for your children out loud it shows them you care for them, and you are setting the most powerful force in the universe (Jesus) loose in their situations.

Takeaways for Pastors

"In 2014, the Bureau of Labor Statistics reported that 124.6 million Americans 16 years and older were single, or 50.2 percent of the population."[1]

Let that sink in. More than half of American adults are single. Is that reflected in your church? Do you have a plan for reaching out to this group in your community? Are you giving them relevant teaching, such as the material from this book? Or do you ignore them?

To youth pastors and young adult pastors, I say don't be scared to discuss the controversial topic of dating. Your members want more than just a pizza party. They are hungry for a game plan on how to date. Feel free to use the ideas from this book as a starting point with your talks and sermons. I am much further along in my faith and life because youth pastors and young adult pastors didn't dodge the difficult questions. You have tremendous influence over the young people in your church. Be the youth pastor who teaches relevant sermons about dating. If you do, you will change their lives for the better.

---

1   http://www.csmonitor.com/USA/Society/2015/0614/
Singles-nation-Why-so-many-Americans-are-unmarried

Acknowledgments

Hayward Broughton designed the cover and did a great job capturing the message of my book.

Corrie Donovan and Jozi Hall both spent many hours going over the text and working with the editing.

Dad and Mom, Burt and Anita Folsom, spent dozens of hours going over this book to make it as clear and readable as possible.

63070017R00141

Made in the USA
Lexington, KY
26 April 2017